MW01067857

# The Cashflow
# Mindset

*Millionaire, Billionaire, & Zillionaire Designs
for Financial Freedom & a Fulfilled Life*

By
## Alan Schnur

Copyright © 2017 Alan Schnur

All rights reserved. No part of this book may be used or reproduced in any manner whatsoever without prior written consent of the authors, except as provided by the United States of America copyright law.

Published by Best Seller Publishing®, Pasadena, CA Best Seller Publishing® is a registered trademark Printed in the United States of America.

ISBN: 978-1-946978-30-1

This publication is designed to provide accurate and authoritative information with regard to the subject matter covered. It is sold with the understanding that the publisher is not engaged in rendering legal, accounting, or other professional advice. If legal advice or other expert assistance is required, the services of a competent professional should be sought. The opinions expressed by the authors in this book are not endorsed by Best Seller Publishing® and are the sole responsibility of the author rendering the opinion.

Most Best Seller Publishing® titles are available at special quantity discounts for bulk purchases for sales promotions, premiums, fundraising, and educational use. Special versions or book excerpts can also be created to fit specific needs.

For more information, please write: Best Seller Publishing®

1346 Walnut Street, #205

Pasadena, CA 91106

or call 1(626) 765 9750

Toll Free: 1(844) 850-3500

Visit us online at: www.BestSellerPublishing.org

# Introduction

My name is Alan Schnur, and I'm a professional real estate investor. I also teach people like you how to invest. Over the last few years, I have bought and sold over $100 million worth of real estate. But it hasn't always been like that. I faced many challenges along the way and paid a high price for the lessons I've learned — including having to live in my office for a year because I couldn't afford an apartment. But I try to take the ups and downs of life in stride. I learned a long time ago that if you're not laughing, you're not learning. And now, I can't wait to share my strategies and methods with you.

Above all, this book is about craftsmanship: how to craft a real estate plan to achieve your goals. My passion to succeed for the benefit of my family and myself drove me to devote whatever free time I could to learning about business and real estate. This single focus turned my fate around and led me to create a Cash Flow Mindset that I now share to give others freedom, choices, and happiness. The ideas that we create together are intended for you, the reader, to have more time for a fulfilling life.

My philosophy is that creating cash flow from a business also leverages another precious commodity: time. We are living in the

most exciting era for wealth creation and business development that
could last for generations. Truly, the world is changing, and so, too,
are the methods used to create wealth. I have uncovered many simple
formulas that work, and most require your involvement for just a
few steps. Everything you do counts, so it's vital to do it right because
at the end of the day, we only have one reputation to rely on. Most
people won't try, and others give up the first time they fail. You can be
different — keep reading to find out how.

## Create Multiple Sources of Income

I have "been there and done that," with expertise developed through
sheer will, in the trenches of experience. I continue to enrich myself
through knowledge and active investing. I've scoured the planet
looking for ideas that are fun and profitable. One of my favorite
methods is real estate. It's not easy to boil down hundreds of hours
of trials, efforts, and failures into a few lines, but I believe that's what
I've done — and that my experiences could be invaluable for you. It
hasn't always been easy, but I've walked away with tons of knowledge
and cash.

While investing in single-family rental houses, I realized I would
have to multiply my income source dramatically to achieve true
financial freedom. I would have to dig deep and start a business that
competed with the very corporation that hired me if I was going to
succeed on my own. This isn't about choosing between your job and
opening a business. It's about doing both of those things at the same
time until you have secured multiple sources of income. When my
first business didn't provide enough satisfaction, I started more. I
also started investing in apartment units. This led to investing in strip
shopping centers, office and medical buildings, and then in a lending
business. Eventually, while running multiple businesses, I had the
pleasure of waking up each morning and deciding which business I
wanted to be part of that day.

Imagine having at least half a dozen to a dozen different sources of income to bounce around, from one to another. Imagine always staying active and busy. I developed a four-tiered model that I will share with you throughout this book. I realized if my dreams were to come true, I would always need to be nimble and versatile to move freely from one idea to another. If one business died, then I had 11 more to help grow. I would no longer depend on just one source of income, either a job working for someone else, or one single business of my own. I knew I would be covered as long as I had systems in place and other options that generated money.

My point is that I do use ideas from real estate, but you don't have to be in the real estate business to benefit from them. I have multiple businesses that feed off each other and have nothing to do with buying and selling property. I found myself in situations that required me to quickly change and grow as the world spun out of control.

I didn't want to be left behind like so many others who worked on and perfected a few ideas, then clung to them rigidly. The problem is that so many businesses today are rapidly becoming outdated and defunct. Even if these businesses have been around for 50 or 100 years, there is no sense in saving a sinking ship if the hole is too big. Personally, I've created over two dozen businesses and spend most of my time with six of them. I found industry hacks and went deep. I maneuver with courage and confidence, and apply my knowledge, as well as what I've built from it and adopted from other sources. Enthusiasm is the key common thread that builds business. The key to success is building systems, sharing your profit, and training people to do what you do.

## Leverage Other People and Share Your Vision

My strategy was simple: I would either go directly to the source, find a cheap deal, and then pay a wholesale price, or I'd pay to have it brought to me at the retail level. My team understood that the goal was to gather assets, so we were either going with a cheap discount store or top-of-the-line shopping mall. Finding real estate was no different than deciding where to buy a pair of sneakers. On the day I purchased my first apartment building, I knew I was finally making my dreams a reality.

Not only did I train others to find me deals, I had the common sense to partner with others who were better at certain tasks than I was, and menial jobs I wasn't good at or didn't want to do. I soon began to earn a more-than-comfortable living through investing in multiple businesses, all because I loved what I was doing and had the freedom to discover new ones.

The day came when I quit my job and started living the life of my dreams — which includes sharing my hard-won know-how with others. Over the years, I've put together an impressive real estate portfolio and built a company that created over 200 jobs. Like a butterfly emerging from a cocoon, I found myself getting into many tough situations and emerging a different person — sometimes with a totally different business than I had planned for.

You need to know four things going into this book:

## 1.  If you can do it one time, you're an expert!

In a short time, I bought more than 2,000 apartment units — 18 apartment complexes — and from this built a property management company that oversaw 7,000 units. Just as a journey of 1,000 miles starts with the first step, my property management experience started from the first house I purchased.

I joke that if you do something one time you're an expert, so it's no surprise that I became an expert by buying hundreds of houses, most of which I still own.

After you face your fears the first time, they can be quickly worn down and conquered. That said, it was not always easy sailing for me.

Someone once said a bend in the road is not the end of the road. How true is this? With all these businesses feeding off each other, my dreams of cash flow, time, and money were all coming to fruition. I never gave up and neither shall you. I became a small hurricane of activity, a force to be reckoned with in the real estate world of my backyard. I am known for creating massive amounts of monthly income from investment properties using creative techniques.

Sometimes it's so easy anyone could do it, and other times it's not, but if you don't *ask*, you don't *get*. We can't take our assets with us when we leave this planet, so these need to be continually recycled. There are many opportunities for getting into this now, and there will continue to be, so ask: why not you? It all starts when you build a base — an asset base.

## 2. It's a good time to borrow money when rates are at historic lows!

All boats rise with the tide when we can borrow money at historic lows with strong demand and a shortage of housing. It's the perfect opportunity to create cash flow and instant, massive wealth. So many people feel they miss out, but I can tell you that there is another real estate bubble about to pop in the commercial markets. Ten years ago, I was on target in anticipating when we would hit bottom, and started buying hundreds of houses and thousands of apartment units.

Once again, assets are about to start changing hands, and as interest rates in the U.S. rise, current owners will need to refinance their current loans. Not all of them will be able to — they will simply send the keys back to the lenders and banks. These assets, by law, must be sold within three years, at any price. I have witnessed this same situation. Decades of wealth and equity will be wiped away, affording us to buy industrial triple-A assets for pennies on the dollar.

### 3.    Buy low, sell high — and spend time with the right people.

I once was part of a group just starting out in the apartment business. Some of us had never completed a single deal and we wanted to learn how others did it. We taught each other and started to network with the right people. I watched this group buy over a billion dollars worth of real estate in less than five years, at half price.

None of us were moguls or massively successful. As a matter of fact, most of us were unemployed or looking to supplement our income so we could quit our day jobs. We were regular folks with families who figured out how to raise money for deals.

One of my greatest achievements during that time was purchasing an apartment building for $1.25 million, which recently appraised for $6 million, instantly creating equity and boosting my net worth. In a separate transaction, I bought an apartment building that brings in over $2.4 million in annual revenues. Think about it: it's actually possible to purchase a business with millions of dollars of revenue.

### 4.    Most doers are stuck because they lack business systems!

Through my unique strategies to close the gap between investing in single-family properties and apartment complexes, I found ways to buy property with no down payment. I will help you do the same to create a more financially sound future. Like many of you, I found the odds against me daunting, and my chances for success, not good.

My journey is about finding a way to discover undervalued assets. I fix things, turn them around, and cash flow them. Some of my biggest lessons came from simply buying a pack of gum for a quarter and selling it for 50 cents at baseball games when I was a kid in upstate New York.

I've worked at making the complex aspects easy to understand and implement. There is a very good reason why most wealthy people have lots of their net worth in real estate. It doesn't take much time out of your day to do this. Many of my ideas and strategies are used in gathering real estate, and I spent most of my years running business systems and managing people, as well. I still do, just not from an office building or cubicle. There are no time clocks in my world anymore, unlike the days when I waited tables to pay for school — and I don't wear a watch for that very reason.

I believe that you're able to connect your experiences and propel yourself into a prosperous future. Most of you are already there. You are just missing the slightest details that make all the difference, just as I was missing them. Here's where you will find them.

# Table of Contents

CHAPTER 1

# 72 Hours
## *(that changed my life forever)*

### September 10, 2001

"5.25, 5.75, 5.25, 5.75, 5, 5, 5, 5, 5. 5! That's 5. 5, 5 and 5.5! Sold! 5.5! 2, 3, 4 hundred! Keep going! 5, 5, 5, 5, 5, 5! Sold 5! Sold 5! Sold 5!" Hundreds of millions of dollars changing hands.

How the hell did I end up here?

Every day for over 10 years, I walked through the complete chaos of commodity trading pits to get to my job. Every day, working for Cantor Fitzgerald, we had to be up by 4 a.m., ready to go and turned on, and we needed to know our positions. On arrival, we would strategize with our partners and customers over the phone.

It was a sport, one we all loved. We'd show up in the pits, and look around to see where our opponents might be buying and selling that day — what kind of positions they were holding onto, and how they were making money — because one thing was clear: they would either take my money or I would take theirs. They had the advantage. Someone needed to be able to turn perceived risk into opportunity.

I saw many things backwards back then, which is why I now know for a fact that hard work and heart are two of the most important attributes for success. I had to memorize numbers in my free time to get ahead in the commodity business. School was over for me, and getting a "b" and a "d" mixed up on a multiple-choice exam now had more serious consequences. Money, food — my very survival — were in real danger. No longer was I the special, gifted child. I had serious disadvantages that I needed to fix quickly. As a master chess player engages in the game with a clear vision going forward, this was going to be a time for me to live out my vision — or be forced to settle for the ordinary.

Sometimes, first thing in the morning, we would need to push through the market and kind of shake the low-hanging fruit from the tree, just to see who was going to be doing what. You needed to test the markets and throw a price out to see if somebody would buy it right away, and then you could set your position up for that spot market — right before things got explosive. Reading people's body language was a necessity. You had to look to their hands for signals, and you needed them to be very clear in their actions. These were some very valuable lessons I carried forward from the commodity market into the real estate market and lending business. I will share some of them in these pages.

We were in the commodity business, working for a large company. We were eager, my partner Stuart and I, for the day when our contracts would be up so we could hang up our own shingle. We didn't know it then, but when I look back, I see that we were developing our Cash Flow Mindset, which is a concept I want to explore in this chapter — an understanding of unlimited financial prosperity with a few basic principles and steps. Stu and I knew that if we could build one successful business, we could then also build 100 successful businesses

— each successful in cash flowing, each revenue stream giving us the passive income we craved so we could stop worrying about the present and simply live in it, and look forward to the future without having to work for someone else.

I will never forget the morning of September 10, 2001. Most of my group was scheduled to take a business trip and after we were done in the pits, we started packing our bags before heading to the airport. But something was wrong. A software product was not ready on time. Forty of us (out of 44 total) were scheduled for the trip, and 38 immediately canceled. Stu and I were the only ones left. As we were about to jump on the elevator, our CEO, Mike, yelled, "Hey, only one of 'youse' guys can go. Just one. The product's not even ready."

I looked at Stu. He looked at me. We both wanted to go out to Los Angeles, Portland, and the West Coast, see some customers and have some nice dinners. But Stu said, "Lisa's pregnant. And if she knew I didn't need to go, she'd never let me live it down."

I thought, *Well, I just moved into a new house and I really need to help my wife unpack* . . . but Stu's need was greater than mine. I shook his hand. "Good luck, and I'll see you in a few days." Before I knew it, I was on my way to Newark Airport, and landed in Portland very late that evening.

## September 11, 2001

We all remember where we were on 9/11.

I awoke to my cell phone ringing, ringing, and ringing. I saw that it was Scott, one of my customers. Scott was a very successful trader, one of the biggest in the industry. We were friends, but it was not like him to call me. I answered.

"Where are you?" he asked.

"Portland, getting ready to see Enron."

"*Phew.*" I could hear the fear in his voice, which was odd, because you do not hear fear coming from commodity traders. He said, "Turn on the TV."

I saw my office building on fire. I sat there, numb and horrified, and watched the smoke. I was frightened for everybody there. I remember that, out of nowhere, another plane hit the building next to mine. From that day forward, life would never be the same. Eight hours later, the casualties were official: 700 out of 1,000 Cantor employees — 40 of my 44 teammates, including my good friend, fellow dreamer, and father-to-be Stu — were dead. I literally felt my spirit fly out of me.

## September 12th

I lost everything. All I had left was my values, ideas, and dreams. My job, my living situation, and my mental state were completely and permanently altered.

My house in Hoboken, New Jersey, was a few blocks from a train station that was no longer there. The backyard of my condo had a clear view of the World Trade Center — no longer there. It was clear that I would need to move with the company because all our offices were gone. It took me years to tell this story, and to this day it's just as heartbreaking. This tragedy prompted my search for meaning and for what was missing in my life: freedom, security, and an understanding of money and its connection to the rest of life.

I continue to remind others about the 72 hours that forever changed the world. This event is one of those times that we always remember, one that reminds us where we were and who we were with when we learned of the attacks. It is a reminder that all of us are alive and surviving. A question emerged for me that day: What will you do with your life, and how deep will you go within yourself to prosper?

I understood how things are easier with money, and harder without it, because I lived through it. I came upon a single idea that made things easier and worked very well for me, and now, my family. I was trapped in a hotel room in Portland on 9/11. Phone calls were next to impossible. I could do little besides reach out to some of the families I knew.

I rewrote the trajectory of my life, all alone in my room. I thought about every human emotion possible, from pain, loss, and grief to success, happiness, and fulfillment. I decided then and there that I would no longer live a small, unnoticed, and regular life. I asked myself one, very important question:

If I had died instead, had I lived? Did I really live?

I did not think so. I had failed, again (see Chapter Five).

Most setbacks are opportunities, and in that moment, I made three pledges: to live larger, play harder, and make a difference in the lives of those around me. This meant going bigger, once and for all. It meant creating cash flow systems and businesses, having children, owning houses and taking vacations, and finding the success I so badly wanted. We all want those kinds of successes in life, but at this point, all I had were ideas. I reached deep down, and my inner self shouted, *I will do it! I will do it!* I call that the Spirit Scream. I wanted to change. I was determined to make all the fallen from that day proud of me, and honor those who helped save lives that day.

## Moving to Texas

When I was finally able to work my way back to New York and regroup with what was left of the company, it was decided that I would move to Texas. I wondered, *what will I tell my wife?* She doesn't speak much English, and we needed to live either in New York or California for her sake — but now we were headed to Pearland, Texas.

Hoboken was cool: Frank Sinatra's hometown and close to Manhattan. It was also a multinational haven for a multicultural marriage. Now, this New York Jew and his Japanese princess had to live in a suburb named for pears! I needed to sweeten the pot, so that week, I asked my princess to marry me, and after she said yes, I broke the news.

As a new Texan, I did what any red-blooded, New York Yankee would do. I bought the largest four-bedroom, two-bath house I could afford, and got busy. I helped Cantor Fitzgerald rebuild. I rented my condo in Hoboken and used the profit, or cash flow, to help pay for our new house. I transitioned fairly well, but how peculiar it all seemed back then. It's true that just when things cannot get any worse, well, you know . . . they always do.

Only three months after our move, Cantor shut my desk down and closed the business. *I lost my job.* Selling the new house would be next to impossible, because what had been a beautiful pear farm across the street was now the beginnings of a 5,000-home subdivision built by the largest U.S. developers.  I now realize that anger over being fired fueled my new businesses — I was forced to move on or starve. I decided that never again would I be baited like a mouse looking for cheese (in this case, a sign-on bonus, stocks, and options in exchange for a long-term employment contract), only to end up in a trap!

The time comes when we need to focus on our strengths and let go of our weaknesses, just as my employer did. Cantor Fitzgerald returned to its core business of stocks and bonds and did away with energy derivative brokering.

But I didn't want to start over! I wanted to build on what I had learned. It seemed silly to gamble on a new idea, but I considered buying a sandwich franchise, deciding against it because the risk of failure was too great. Instead, I decided to copy the exact business model that put me out of a job. I began to see the proverbial light at the end of the tunnel. As my own boss, I could eventually hire someone to run the business while I focused on creating another. I understood brokering and decided to set up my own shop. I didn't want to start over, but that's what I did.

At Radio Shack, I found two telephones on sale for $39.95. I will never forget looking at them and scratching my head. Did I really need 18 lines? As I considered my options, it occurred to me that 18 symbolizes so much in life. In the Jewish faith, it represents the gift of life and good luck. Numerous Asian cultures have the concept that a business somehow associated with 18 will prosper.

My thinking was simple: *Let's go! 18 times everything I want to do. 18 phone lines, 18 more chances of making money.*

I bought the phones and ordered 18 lines from the phone company that day. Living bigger meant going bigger, and going bigger meant growing into the Cash Flow Mindset that I was creating. Those were the goals I came up with on 9/11, alone with my thoughts in that hotel room. Going bigger meant getting bigger. No more living a small life. *I will do it, I will do it, I will do it!* my spirit continued screaming.

## When Opportunity Knocks

*(let her in...)*

I was now in business, but I asked myself, *what am I going to broker or sell? All of my teammates are dead.* I had to get serious. Make some decisions. *How am I going to make money so my wife and I can prosper?* I had nothing to guide me so I simply made it up. Turns out, I was an innovator of an hourly power trading product that could trade 24 hours a day. I would make money in my sleep.

Cash Flow Mindset = Making money in your sleep.

This is how I designed it: You have a marketplace with buyers and sellers that want to buy low and sell high — like when making bets and playing the lottery. They can buy only during two times of the day (basically, morning and night). I decided to change that. I thought, *why can't they just buy hourly power when they need it?* I created a product that all banks and utility companies across North America could trade.

And guess what? They had to call me to transact and trade.

I started my business in my home office (in my house), and hired people. I decided that if I could convince people that my vision of the future was workable, I could use my Cash Flow Mindset. *If I can do it, I can show others how to do it. I can teach them how to yield markets and how to speak to my customers.* Before long, I ran out of phone lines.

I will never forget a call from my friend Larry. He said, "Alan, I know what you're doing, and we're breaking down a trading floor right now. We have a lot of equipment to sell you." I always believed in building a bigger business, and going somewhere: moving and shaking. I balanced, pivoted, and moved. Larry had the goods, so he had my attention!

"I'm interested, but frankly, I don't have a lot of money."

"We will make a deal."

He drove over in this white van. He opened the door, and I saw around $250,000 worth of trading phone equipment. My eyes lit up. I said, "Larry, all I have is $15,000."

He said, "Sure."

Before I knew it, he started unloading the equipment into my office: huge phone servers, big computer systems, and yards of cables. I said, "Larry, what do you do with all that cable?"

"It's for the servers."

"Servers?"

"You'll have to put the servers in another room because they get very hot."

The only available room was a nursery, so that's where we put them. Larry snaked the cables from the nursery through the ceiling crawl space and into my office. I heard an awful crash and ran downstairs to find that he had fallen from the scaffolding, through the ceiling, and onto the floor. *Oh my God. Is he dead?* He was not. I helped him up.

I looked up at the massive hole with insulation spilling out, and asked myself, *What in the world am I going to tell my wife?* Despite the mess, we were able to install a massive trading room in my house in Pearland, Texas.

Once the servers were on, we could never turn them off. Phones rang 24 hours a day. They woke my wife up at about 4:00 one Saturday morning. She started poking me, wanting me to wake up and get upstairs to make money.

I said, "What?" She was speaking in Japanese.

My morning brain thought, *Guess I'd better get to work!*

I grabbed my robe to cover my tighty-whities and headed out. I picked up the trading phones, and it was just explosive. It was Matt from Pacific Gas and Electric. He said, "Hey, Alan, water's down, we need 500 megs. Go get us—" and he started yelling all these orders. Before I knew it, half the day was gone and we were literally buying and selling over $250 million worth of electricity — probably up to a half a billion that day for Matt's utility company — all from my little house in Pearland.

I looked in the mirror and realized, *Wow, this is turning into a business!* I was charged up. The phones never stopped ringing for the next 10 years. I thought I had a cash flow business, but in fact I was just an entrepreneur who had more or less created a job for himself. There was a lot of profit, but I had to be present to make sure that it came in. Eventually, I grew dissatisfied with that. I felt like an employee, always feeling that if I did not show up, the revenues would not be there. My gut told me it was time to get out. I was always looking over my shoulder because you never know when the next plane will hit.

CHAPTER 2

# Millionaire Mindset

I believe that the more things we try, the greater our chances of succeeding. It's so important to throw mud onto the wall, see what sticks, and work with what is left. I was in this brokerage business and doing very well, but always felt that the end was near; I needed to diversify and have multiple income streams. I chose real estate. Because I already had one rental from my Hoboken days, I thought I could expand upon my knowledge. I also chose this because I wanted something truly passive. With real estate, I could dream about collecting checks in the mail while watching the asset grow.

I started buying marketing programs over the Internet, along with those late-night television infomercial kits. I finally visited a local club called The Rich Club, and watched and learned from the world's greatest speakers and educators. The common thread was clear: you had to take action to make cash flow work.

Eventually, it was time to put the books down and get out in the field. So, you know what? I bought all their stuff and it worked. My goal was simple: I was looking for life-changing cash, and had found a way to get it.

Millionaire thinking means understanding that creating income is your job; you pay your expenses and what's left is profit. This is the fundamental process that we are going to build on in this book, and single-family house investments are a perfect example. It's pure and raw. You collect rent, pay bills, and your profit is what's left. If you rent the house, then your profit is your cash flow. If you flip it, your profit is your gain.

That first Saturday, I kissed my wife good-bye and told her what I was up to, and that I would have to pay $40 a month to be in The Rich Club. When I got there, I found that I could buy a year-long pass for $400. I reasoned to myself: *I had told my wife I would spend $40, but I will go ahead and charge $400 to save $80.*

I couldn't wait to see what The Rich Club was all about. On the stage in the main room, a gentleman told stories about buying houses for 50 cents on the dollar, and then flipping them to make quick cash or build a rental portfolio. This was exactly what I was looking for: a way to create passive income. Lo and behold, at that moment I had my new idea: I could build a large rental portfolio. I'll never forget when the speaker said, "When you own the real estate, there is very little left to do. And that's why you have enough time in a day to own as much as you want. "

I spend the morning listening to everyone. After a while, I had to go down the hall to the bathroom. This gentleman, Dennis, was set up in the hallway, selling one-on-one instruction, and coaching/ mentoring on single-family

houses, rehabbing, and building a rental portfolio. We chatted, and he seemed to know a lot. He gave the impression that he had the knowledge to help jump-start the education I so desperately wanted.

I was in, but there was a hitch. Joining cost $8,000. *Oh, boy!* I had already shelled out 10 times the money I had told my wife I would spend that morning, but you know what? I pulled out my credit card and charged $8,000 to learn how to buy single-family houses.

*Oh, man,* I thought on the drive home. *What am I going to tell my wife?* We did not have much income. I reminded her that the biggest factor holding us back was our fear, and that we would have to buy our first property to get over it. She was alarmed, but after we bought our first investment house (for $23K), fixed it up, and rented it out, we never looked back.

What that taught us was that if we could buy one, then we could buy 10. And if we could buy 10, then we could buy 100. I saw that my Cash Flow Mindset would make us money even while we slept. I also joked that my wife spending more time at Home Depot than the Galleria would create less heartburn for me.

## The Four R's

1. The golden rule came out of that $8,400 investment:
2. Rehab
3. Rent
4. Refi
5. Repeat

We bought that first house for $23,000, fixed it up, and rented it. I bought another the following month, and we had over 150 houses just 10 years later. We sold some, but we also built a rental portfolio. This is the Millionaire, Billionaire & Zillionaire Mentality that I want to share with you. If you can by one, then you can buy 10. If you can buy 10, then you can buy 100. If you can buy 100, then you can buy 1,000 — a process we will go over soon. By this time, I was developing my Cash Flow Mindset system.

I also realized that it made no sense to hoard money in the bank. I needed to exchange that money for assets, which would have a different value than mere currency. Paper money doesn't grow as fast as a hard asset, such as a house. Paper money doesn't cash flow like a house, or grow in value like a house, either. I developed a mindset for converting dollars into housing units. A dollar of paper money comes into my pocket and a hard asset, such as a house or apartment unit, comes out. At the same time, I helped people sell their houses.

Most were in poor condition and needed money to fix them up. But that's where I added the most value to the community. I replaced rundown houses with a little castle inside my oasis of prosperity. They were transformed from eyesores to houses anyone would be proud to call home. I learned quickly that if I didn't have time to find my own properties, I could pay others — a broker or property flipper — to bring them to me. This didn't matter as long as the investment was within my guidelines for cash flow and equity. I would pay an analyst if I didn't have time to delve deep into the numbers. I paid an assistant to handle all the small details important to the deal.

Don't let "I don't have time" be an excuse. If you're going to get ahead, you need to build a team and leverage your time, especially if you're creating a hold strategy as I did. Houses are one of my dependable cash flows — one of the many rivers filling my ocean. The cash from houses was enough to sustain me. But I wanted more.

## A Winning Hand

Just as we know the seasons will change, we know that economic recessions are inevitable. When everyone is making money, things are great, but when that's not the case, people begin to fight. For me, this was like the plane hitting the building all over again. The images never leave me. This was my signal to sell my brokerage business to my partners. *Time to clear my mind and move on.* I wanted to focus on real estate and build my Cash Flow Mindset, my multiple income streams, and my rental portfolio. But first, I booked a trip to Tokyo, where I always go to clear my mind.

I will never forget our first week in Japan. We were visiting my in-laws (Gigi and Baba, grandma and grandpa in Japanese), sitting in this very, very small room, about to feast on a huge platter of sushi. I wanted to check my email first, so I sat down at their ancient computer and logged on to AOL. I heard the familiar "You've got mail," and boy, did I have mail! One of my bankers had just taken back 25 houses from a failed investor, and wanted to sell them all to me.

I was trying to act very cool and calm, not only because I was on sabbatical in Japan, but also because I knew there was no way my wife, Takako, would let me buy so many houses, site unseen.

I casually asked her if she could take me to the American Embassy so I could buy a house. You might not know what a Jewish white lie is, but it's the idea is that if something serves the greater good and benefits everyone, it is okay to fudge the truth a little. I intended to buy all 25 houses, but buying even one would have been a problem since she knew I had not seen it.

The documents arrived from the bank via email the next day, and we went to the American Embassy. I was sure she would figure out that I was carrying paperwork for more than just one house, so I suggested she would have more fun at Tsukiji, which is probably the world's best seaport market, and that I would meet her there for lunch. I remember walking into the Embassy, meeting the notary, and having all those pages stamped. At that point, the deal was done. All I had to do was drop my pages off at a FedEx or DHL, and the houses would be mine.

On the way to Tsukiji, it hit me. *I just got 25 houses for $30,000 each, and they're easily worth $75,000 in a bad market, and for sure over $100,000 in a good market. I did the math: 45,000 times 25 . . . that's north of a million dollars of equity I just created on my balance sheet!* I decided not to tell my wife because she might spend the money as if it were in our pockets instead of just on paper.

Another important fact is that I had just created a $5,000-a-month cash flow. That's exactly what I set out to do: gain $5,000 a month cash flow on top of what I already made. This might not be enough to suit you; maybe you want $10,000, $15,000, $50,000, or $100,000. However, if you can do it once, you can do it 10 times. If you can do it 10 times, you can do it 100 times. If you can do it 100 times, you can do it 1,000 times. It's up to you to decide how much you want to make.

Of course, I was not satisfied with an additional $5,000 a month in passive income. I needed to find more houses. If you own a business or are buying a house, it's all the same regarding leveraging your time. We all have 24 hours in a day — that's 1,440 minutes. If you commit just 1% of your time (14.4 minutes per day) to creating a cash flowing future, you could absolutely own a business in less than 90 days.

I sat down at the sushi bar in the fish market. It was one of those cold, gray places, and it smelled of fish and burning logs. Most surfaces were wet, and a damp mist filled the air. As my wife poured me a little sake, I wondered, *How lucky did I just get and how can I do that again? Do I just hope and pray, or can I make something happen?* Over my shoulder to my left were a bunch of houses, and to my right, apartment buildings. My head started spinning. *Houses, apartment buildings. Houses, apartment buildings. I just bought 25 houses.* I had a huge a-ha moment. *That's what I will do for an encore — start buying apartment buildings.*

That night, back in Tokyo, I researched apartment buildings online. There was one for sale next to the 25 houses I had just bought. I thought it would be a perfect combination. I bought it and loved it. Then I bought many more. I could scale up! I could scale up my Cash Flow Mindset as large as I wanted. That's the thing about real estate, and what took me so long to create the Cash Flow Mindset. It needs to be based on a re-investible idea so that larger groups can buy from you and sell to you.

## Cash Flow Mindset

What is the Cash Flow Mindset? I break it down into five parts:

1. Set your cash flow business up or invest in one.
2. Make sure you get payments 90-120 days later, every month.
3. Buy what you need with the cash flow.
4. Send out your warriors — your cash flow, your dollars.
5. Reinvest what's left over to create more cash flow businesses.

I don't know if you will buy houses or apartments or start a business, but let me tell you where this all started for me: with a dream of starting my own business so I could enjoy freedom, independence, growth, and unlimited income. Many of us look for shortcuts. This was my problem, too.

I did not have the tools in the toolbox, I did not have the software for the computer, and I did not have the recipe for the cake. I spent years trying to shortcut the process and got nowhere, fast. I had to go through these phases and make the connections on my own to really get it. I had the worst jobs early on: selling my family's line of shirts in a shopping mall and at swap meets and flea markets up and down the East Coast. I thought if I just sold enough, I could end up owning the shopping mall. This was not even possible.

I then spent years on Wall Street. I made cold calls to 1,000 people a week. I thought I would miraculously end up owning the brokerage shop. Of course, that never happens. I was miserable. Then, I fantasized about being an international businessman. I didn't know what I going to sell, but I liked the idea. I opened an office on John Street in the

Financial Center in downtown New York. I had no business plan, but was just chasing dreams. This time, I truly ran out of money, again and again and again. I had to choose between keeping my office or my apartment, because I could no longer afford both.

Being the entrepreneur that I was and given the path I was on, of course I gave up the apartment and moved into the office, which was 250 square feet. The chair to my desk was a futon that became my mattress. I can still picture it today. I spread out the futon and put my head under the desk to keep the light out. We taped sheets across the window that made up the exterior wall to try to keep out the light.

I joined a gym so I could shower in the mornings. I sneaked out very early so no one would figure out what was going on. All along, I was just scheming, dreaming, and planning on making it big in business.

I realized my dreams were empty. I had nothing to back them up. *Why do some people succeed and others do not? Why are my dreams failing to come true?* I figured out mine were empty, baseless, and mostly fantasy. Most of us only hope — <u>we do not do</u>. We do not take action. This was when I identified my problem: too much hope and not enough action. To remedy this, I took the lowest position available at a commodity brokerage firm. I wanted to learn something inside out. I realized my weaknesses and committed to improving them. I watched and learned, determined to becoming the best.

When they told me I was going to be a lunch boy, I was not just any lunch boy; I was the best lunch boy. When they told me I was going to be an errand boy, I was not just any errand boy; I was the best errand boy. When they told me I was going to be a board boy and write down numbers, I would not just be any board boy, I would be the best board boy. Being the best finally landed me a seat on the desk at this commodity brokerage shop. I learned quickly, and the lessons started early.

Every step forward — win, lose, or draw — was a l
toward success. I stopped being angry about my failures a... starteu
being more humble, modest, and accepting of myself. It was not until I
started paying attention to how things worked and connected with one
another that I developed the systems and processes that have worked
so well for me and others — what I call the Billionaire Mindset.

## Just Another 60-year Plan?

I want to share a secret. It's about my second family, my money
warriors. They are warriors because they had better come back, and
bring more than they left with, because this is all about cash flow —
the Cash Flow Mindset; not another 60-year plan that says it takes
60 years to make a million dollars. A Cash Flow Mindset is universal
thinking among the well off, as it should be for the rest of us. Set up your
cash flow business or invest in one. Buy what you need with the cash
flow; send your warriors out. Reinvest what is left into more cash flow
businesses. Your money warriors don't care about your age, lifestyle,
or education. They only care about respect and reasonableness. Treat
them right and they are yours forever. Treat them wrong and they will
be gone twice as fast as it took to get them.

Another reason this is such a powerful concept is because when
I'm thinking in terms of an army, I withdraw myself, along with my
emotions, when making business decisions. I have learned I make
better choices when I'm thinking clearly and with little emotion. We
can have one or the other working at any given time, meaning that
when emotions are up, our clear-thinking process is down, and when
the thinking process is up, emotions are down.

I don't want to be on the 60-year plan to make my first million.
Who would? The 60-year plan means 20 years of schooling plus 40
years of work. That's not for me, and it's probably not for you. I believe
our abilities are bigger than we can imagine. I believe in life-long

education and hanging around the right people. I believe in a Cash Flow Mindset of creating business systems that will free you from the ordinary path.

Farmers often say that it takes seed, time, and harvest. It works the same way with money, too! Execute your plan. Pick your business. Find a specialty. For me, this was my first job in the commodity markets, after which I created my own business, and then trained and hired others. Then, I created business systems. I executed the same formula in the housing business, and I did it again in the management business. This system works in all businesses. It can work for you.

CHAPTER 3

# Billionaire Mindset

W hat is the Billionaire Mindset, and how do we acquire it? I developed some principles from all the things I did that put me on the path. For me, it all started with my first investment house, because I always had this burning question that I carried around with me: Why do some people make five, 50, or 5,000 times more money than others?

In the large corporation where I worked, most of us in the same division did the same thing. Years later, I learned that our salaries differed wildly, from $125,000 to $300,000 per employee. I saw the same trend in the real estate business. I saw people making more money in commercial real estate in 10 days than I could make in my lifetime.

This time, I identified the components at work in this phenomenon: time, leverage, and multiple sources of income and cash flow. This was a new game for me, and I loved playing it! In the single-family housing business, the formula for making money was simple. All I needed to do was take my income and subtract my expenses, and I would be left with a profit. But as the assets got bigger — for example, from houses to apartment complexes — I quickly learned that I needed to leverage more and take on more debt.

When handled responsibly, debt becomes a currency — a currency of the rich! In fact, debt has benefits that can be more valuable than cold, hard cash. As the costs of materials rise, so do the values of my properties. My debt is slowly paid down by tenants, but more importantly, I can take advantage of cheap money, rising inflation, and multiple tax incentives.

## The Tie Was Cut...

*(I'd make millions)*

When I closed my first account as a stockbroker on Wall Street, the guys cut my necktie in half, as is the tradition. This signifies that if you can close one account, you can close thousands. I applied that idea to buy a lot of real estate.

So, when I saw I could buy one house, I realized I could buy 10. When I bought 10, I saw I could buy 100. If I bought 100, I could buy 1,000. I applied that concept, the Billionaire Mindset, to apartment buildings. Again, I bought one apartment building. If I had one unit, I could have 10 units. If I could have 10 units/doors, I could have 100 units/doors. If I had 100, I could have 1,000.

Then I realized I was truly breaking through and growing into a Cash Flow Mindset that gave me a new lifestyle from the asset pool I was creating. I was continually setting real estate goals and reviewed them each morning. It was like tapping into a treasure chest each day, and new ideas and investments would appear in my mind. My goals were aggressive and kept me motivated and on track to building a larger cash flowing mindset. They kept rolling in, which was a fantastic way of measuring my growth.

You see, once I bought 1,000 apartment units, I dreamt of 2,000 units. I pushed through that and I bought 2,000 units. From there, I decided to push beyond what I believed was possible for me. Using the same concepts, I started buying office buildings, medical plazas, and retail shopping centers/strips. In this case however, I calculated using square footage. If I could buy a 5,000-square-foot center, then maybe next time I would buy a 10,000-square-foot center, and then a 15,000-square-foot center. I kept pushing myself out of my comfort zone and forcing myself to grow. I was able to measure my progress by square footage, because if I could buy 15,000 square feet, then I could buy 20,000 square feet. If I could buy 20,000 square feet, then I could buy 40,000 square feet and 50,000 square feet. Currently, I am looking at 100,000-square-foot shopping centers.

All this started from the purchase of one, $23,000 house and now I was looking at $23 million in investments. I didn't even have the money for my first deal. I borrowed money to buy and fix up that house, and then rented it and created cash flow. I realized that if I could make $100 from one single-family house, I could make tens of thousands of dollars, and even millions of dollars, by buying 50,000-square-foot shopping centers.

I'd seen traders in the commodity business all around me do exactly this. They may call that pyramiding, taking one brick and making two out it, and then doubling that: from two to four bricks, four to eight bricks, eight to 16 bricks, 16 to 32, 32 to 64, and so on. As you can see, the numbers can get very large, very quickly, in pyramiding.

I've also used these ideas while playing blackjack in casinos. Maybe someone starts off with $100 and wins. Now they have $200 on the table. They pull back their $100 and are then playing with house money that is not technically theirs, and they have protected their original investment. They have an incredible defense. They cannot lose what they started with because it's already off the table. Again, they can pyramid their $100 to $200, to $400, to $800, to $1,600.

I decided to use that strategy in real estate. But this time, it would be different. If I flipped a property and sold it, that would be an event, a job, and a lot of work. If I decided to hold and cash flow, what I call an ongoing process.

Once you begin implementing these pyramiding systems and the doubling and multiplying effect, you can add another system, called asset swapping. This has worked tremendously well for me. When I bought my first house and decided to buy another and another, and ramped up to 10 houses, I realized that I could speed up the process if I turned in those 10 houses to buy a small apartment building. Once I had that small apartment building, to speed up the process, I could then go buy a mid-sized apartment building. Again, I could turn that mid-sized apartment building into a much larger apartment building. Then, I could take that apartment building and turn it into a strip shopping center, and then I could turn that into a medical plaza.

I swapped apples for oranges and oranges for zucchinis. I kept the velocity of money moving, which is another important principle to mention here: opportunities are everywhere, and if necessary, you should always keep the money moving.

## Learn to See Opportunity Everywhere

My international travels taught me at a young age that growth does not always arrive in your backyard. In real estate markets, I found that when we get overheated and prices are too high, we sometimes have to make a choice: we can either wait for the market to correct itself, or we can go somewhere else. Waiting can take too long, sometimes more than a decade if you are not sure where you are in a real estate market. I decided to move around from state to state.

What I saw living outside the United States, in what we call emerging markets, was that other economies that are not as far advanced as the U.S. sometimes catch up quickly. If it was China, or

Thailand, or India, if it was Israel, or Europe, they all correct themselves, and they all move at their own pace. The lesson here is that you don't always have to be patient waiting for your backyard to experience massive growth or massive decline. You can go somewhere else. This is exactly what I've done with my money.

Sometimes, we see the housing market as simultaneously strong and overpriced. We also find that opportunities in apartment buildings are priced more right now, which is why I just sold a dozen apartment complexes and bought a half dozen strip shopping centers. My returns are safer, stronger, and more attractive than if I were about to go out and buy houses and apartment buildings today. That leads me to my next point.

## Keep the Money Moving

The question we must ask ourselves regarding the velocity of money is, "What is the best use of my money?" Money supports our lifestyle and happiness. And let's face it: as we get older, we become less physical, and lose the strength of our youth. It becomes more important to save, create, and gather works for us as we enjoy life more, as we slow down a little to smell the flowers and perhaps rest a little more than before. We need to discover the best use for our money: where to put it, and where to weigh the averages.

I evolved into a professional investor, a good steward of money, which most people are not. It's often said that you are either red or blue — that you think like an engineer or a salesperson; but in either case, one revenue stream of income is too risky to depend on. The best way to diversify is by multiplying streams of cash flow by adding a variety of businesses to your portfolio.

How many houses do you need to pay for your freedom? How many doors/units of an apartment building do you need for financial security? And how many shopping centers do you need to buy for unlimited financial prosperity? When I built houses, I learned that all the money was made in the development phase. You will win with a pencil, paper, and a plan. Changes in the field cost a fortune!

A well-balanced real estate portfolio would be:

25% mix of houses,
25% mix in apartment complexes,
25% mix of shopping center/strip centers, and
25% mix in stocks, commodities, and bonds.

Every so often, rebalance this pie chart. Let's say stocks appreciate to become not just 25% of my portfolio, but 30% or 35%. I rebalance and recalibrate it by selling 10% or 15% of those stocks. Then, I look at the other portfolios and make a decision: will I put this 10% or 15% into houses, apartments, or shopping centers? I weigh all the pros and cons and find where the velocity of money will work best. This is implementing business systems that allow us to create multiple income streams.

I have money coming in every month from stock dividends and houses, and through the cash flow of apartments and shopping centers. If one area of real estate gets bad, I can rely on the others.

I'm always implementing business systems and creating new ones. The system is what's important at the beginning of the process. It trains you to be more prepared and financially independent. It allows you to spend more time away from the actual process as you grow and expand, and it protects you in unforeseen circumstances, such as if you get sick. If the right systems, procedures, processes, and people are in place, things should continue without interruption. It's like learning how to swim — eventually you swim farther from the edge and trust the process.

CHAPTER 4

# Zillionaire Mindset

A wise man once told me that there are easy ways of making money, and difficult ways. He said it was my job to find what came easily to me. This idea will be part of your Zillionaire Mindset thinking process. I applied this thought to real estate and decided some ways of making money were easier than others. When I was in the single-family house business, it felt like I was always fighting to get my rent. Then I tried the apartment business, and it was a little easier, although it sometimes was a struggle. That is why I transitioned into shopping centers using my Zillionaire thinking cap.

I started controlling larger properties with the use of leverage (other people's money) with significant residual income spitting off from the properties. All I had to do was follow this formula of seven steps that can rapidly increase our net worth. This is a process I use in the shopping center/retail business.

## Zillionaire Thinking:

1. Increase revenue

2. Decrease expenses

3. Increase profit

4. Decrease the cap rate

5. Sell the deal

6. Find cheap debt

7. Buy another property

I found the shopping center business easier and more interesting than residential housing. I liked working with tenants that were worth a billion or a zillion dollars. I liked the fact that they took care of their storefronts. They fixed things. They paid their taxes, and when taxes went up, they paid more. They paid for insurance. They basically paid for everything.

I looked at all the real estate across the United States and scratched my head. Storefronts located right on the edge of major intersections are known as "hard corners," and are worth so much money. The ground underneath is lucrative in and of itself. Realizing this led me to develop a new idea: Legacy Investing. I saw all of these popular, neighborhood destination centers, and I liked the fact that the tenants are geographically locked into their location. If they pick up and leave, most of their customers won't support the move. The convenience factor is more important than goods and services when it comes to shopping centers.

Shopping centers can create perpetual income for you and those who follow you. Location, quality of tenants, and traffic should be able to withstand recessions and other economic downturns. In good times, prices and rates rise, with the debt paid down by your tenants. You will have the choice to cash out of the deal or continue paying down the loan and cash flowing. Eventually, when you and your partners have been paid back a return on your investment (ROI), your partners will forever be grateful. Raising cash for deals takes on a new meaning. I turn money away all the time, because I can raise millions with a few phone calls. Magic capital always appears when you wave your wand!

I took the conversation deeper. In the house business, I focused on profits. In the apartment business, I was more interested in using debt and leverage. And in the shopping center business, I've added the component of depreciation. Of course, this can be used in all stages of real estate ownership; however, it just made more sense for me to focus on this part of the wealth equation as my investors and I became more knowledgeable and sophisticated. The bigger my business grew, the more tax write-offs my investors and I needed.

Trophy properties — ones that last forever in your real estate portfolio — can continually make money for you and your family. They make money while you travel around the world, or send family members to private school. Whatever you choose, the cash flow from these properties continues. This is the Zillionaire Mindset business system: reinvesting and reinventing yourself while staying ahead of the curve.

This reminds me of a video game I play. The player sets up massive rock catapults against an invading army. Setting everything up takes time, but when you cut the cords and launch the flaming boulders, the time invested becomes leveraged and does your work for you for the rest of the round.

Billions of people are going online. Some were able to make $100,000 last year, but the real question is, can we turn our $100,000 into a $1 million? Or will it end up being just $100 when new laborers come online, and disruptive technologies are introduced? With this category of real estate, none of this matters, because your tenants will continue to pay, and what is left over will continue to provide you with cash flow.

I think it is imperative to push ourselves into new ventures every five years or so. Perhaps this is why I found myself in a small business, and graduated into the housing business, then moved into the apartment business. I found myself buying office and medical buildings, renting to doctors, dermatologists, chiropractors, and dentists. Then I found myself in the shopping center business, where I'd rent out to brands like AT&T, T-Mobile, Game Stop, Pizza Hut, Domino's Pizza, Subway, and local and national banks. I rented to all of these national names located in what I call local destination shopping centers.

Building a business and switching every five years keeps things fun and exciting. You cannot wait to wake up every morning to see what is new and what the day will bring for you. There will be bumps and bruises along the way, and it is important to get up as fast as possible when you fall. Getting up itself will prepare you for your transition into your next venture, your new business, or your new piece of real estate. The transition makes you tough, and ready for whatever might come.

Another part of the Zillionaire Mindset is teaching and giving back. Just yesterday, I spent time with a student. We had a strong connection as we spoke about shopping centers, strategies, and ideas that would help him generate passive income, and spend more time with his family and doing what he wants to do, not what he needs to do. It was so exciting to have this conversation, and to share the knowledge gained from the years I spent connecting the dots for myself.

You see, time passes no matter what you do or what happens around you. If you can continue to collect assets that appreciate, build, and grow through time, as you get older, your assets become stronger. Cash flow becomes larger, and perhaps you can then slow down. The idea is to work less for money, and spend more time living a fulfilling life. Like the catapult in the video game, my money becomes the ultimate army, with each dollar a warrior.

Each dollar is put to work for me. Whether it's a small business, house, apartment complex, or shopping center, my dollars, my money warriors, are out there fighting while I am doing something else,. I might be hiking Mount Kilimanjaro in Tanzania or exploring the bush in Australia on the back of a camel. My point is that your money warriors are out there working on your behalf. You are not working for them. You will understand this when you truly understand how business systems work, and how to connect your own dots. Most importantly, you will learn this when you understand how to truly enjoy life, so you can do what you want to do, and not what you need to do.

CHAPTER 5

# Dust Off & Get Back in the Game

This story is taken from a speech about money I gave at Harvard University. I lost a lot of money, and then made a lot of money. In life, when things are going well, there tends to be a bump in the road, and then things tend to fall apart quickly. We need to pick ourselves back up if possible, dust ourselves off, and get back into the game. We must fix and improve our situation.

I have made a lot of money, and lost it, and made a lot of money, and lost it. Each time, I refined myself, and finally had some businesses that were successful and gave me the opportunity to make a lot of money again. At one time I ran a small business, a brokerage shop of around 30 or 40 employees, over a five-year run. We had around $50 million in revenue. Our first year brought just a little over $200,000 in sales. I learned how to create business systems, get better at what I was doing, hire the right people, trust the right people, and trust the process.

Another time, I ran a $100 million real estate portfolio, which began when I bought that first house for $23,000. But the story got exciting years earlier, when I spent a semester at the University of Amsterdam near the end of my college career. I took a psychology class that met in a coffee house. I did the things that one probably should do in that kind of class, in a coffee shop in Amsterdam. I knew one thing for sure: my schooling was about to end.

After that, I did what most college students do: fly back to mom and dad and try to figure out how to get a job. People in this situation often live rent-free, with mom and dad taking care of them while they transition from college to a real job and life after college. I didn't have any plans other than knowing I would have my own business.

My family was in the clothing trade and I grew up selling clothing, so I decided to continue with what I knew. I made $100 a day traveling from shopping mall to shopping mall along the East Coast, setting up a huge canopy in the middle of the mall and spending 12 or 13 hours trying to persuade women to buy my products. I told them how beautiful they would look in the clothing, showed them a few selections, and tried to convince them to try some on. I knew if I could show them a few great choices, they would buy an item or two.

What really kept me going was the goal that I had written down (you really need to write things down in life): to save $10,000. Over many weeks, I placed hundred-dollar bills into my safety deposit box.

That was the highlight of my week: driving to the bank, going inside, opening the box, and adding a few hundred dollars. I came up with a plan for what I would do with my first $10,000, how would I invest it, and how would I create my first business:

- I would take an office on John Street in New York City's financial district.
- I would rent a cheap room.

- I would get a computer and phone line.
- I would start an import/export business.

I did not know what I would import or export, but I was certain I would have a computer and phone line, and an office. I would be in business. I researched some ideas and learned that the government had programs for anyone trying to establish relationships with other countries to secure products for import or export.

For the next few months, I attended networking meetings at night. I realized that the $10,000 I saved wasn't nearly enough. I had to make some hard choices. *Do I give up my apartment, or do I give up my office where I had a chance to build my own business?* I decided to live out of my office, which was around 250 square feet and inside an office building. I would have been thrown out if anyone found out, so I had to sneak in early and sneak out very late.

I joined a gym in the World Trade Center. I was in great shape because I had to walk there all the time just to take a shower. Half the time I didn't even work out, but it was one of my hangouts, because that was all I could afford to do. The import/export idea was not working. I was quickly going broke.

Like so many recent college graduates who are not so sure what they will do in life, I signed up for a graduate-level course, an import/export class held in the World Trade Center. I remember listening intently as the instructor, Tony, explained how Venezuela was poised to be the next big market. The only complication was that the corrupt border patrol made importing and exporting very difficult.

He said that if we wanted to build a business in Venezuela, we needed to set up our own factories there, so we would not have to deal with the border patrol. I thought to myself, *I will do it. I will do it. I will do it.* It burst out, the spirit scream which we all have. I immediately started a business plan and hired Tony as a consultant that week.

Within a week or two, I had a marketing plan, performer, and business plan. I needed to raise $500,000. My dwindling bank account had $2,000. *Only $498,000 to go . . .*

Late one night, I wrote down the names of all the people I knew who might be able to help. *My sister dated a few rich guys when I was growing up, so maybe I can call them up.* I got their phone numbers and called them.

I decided to be in the soap and chemical business, and created what I call my Stadium Pitch. This is what you would say if you were standing in center field at a stadium and have two minutes to tell the 20,000 people in front of you what you want to do.

I put labels on my products and pitched my business idea at the local golf club. The next thing I knew, I had 501,000! I did not get all $500,000 from this group, but I got most of it from them, and friends and family kicked in, too. I was down to my last thousand dollars, but I was set to go to Venezuela. I was ready to manufacture soap and clean up South America.

Just before I left, I learned that you can't wire money to Venezuela. *Why didn't I know that earlier?* I stuffed $300,000 in a fanny belt and strapped it around my waist. Boy, was I nervous walking through customs! I will never forget landing in Caracas, the capital, around 1 a.m., just happy to be there. I thought, *I will create this business! Life is great*!

Uniformed men with AK-47s were stationed throughout the airport. Even kids had these guns. At that point it dawned on me how much trouble I could get into by sneaking this much money into the country. I filled out the forms, sailed through customs, and took a taxi to my hotel without ever being stopped. Now that I am older and wiser, I realize this was absolutely insane.

Once in my room, I decided to listen to music, something I often did to calm my anxiety and help the creative juices flow again. I realized I had a huge task: hiring workers for a 5,000-square-foot warehouse.

I started interviewing accountants and chemical engineers. The whole plan came together and before I left, I realized, *I just gave a $50,000 check to a consultant who got me into this mess in the first place.* I ordered a bunch of chemicals and other ingredients, an agitator, a mixer, and all the equipment. Eight weeks into the process, there was no container.

I called my instructor and employee, Tony, but got no answer. I called the school and they told me he was gone. Later, some of my classmates laughed, saying, "Didn't you hear? It was a Ponzi scheme. He got a few students hooked and everybody was buying something from each other." I was the only one who had actually gone to Venezuela to make things happen. I was the last guy who did not have seat when the music stopped in this game of musical chairs. Getting ripped off for $500,000 was a rude awakening.

I panicked at needing to come up with a new plan. I hired an agent to help me buy equipment (which never arrived). The next thing I knew, he took me to a manufacturing plant that was going out of business and leaving the country. I was able to buy all the equipment I needed, and a lot more, for pennies on the dollar and ship it all to my new warehouse. I now had a state-of-the-art warehouse and was off and running!

Seeing my plan come together was very exciting. I had a sales force and engineers and accountants, and distribution lined up. Slowly, we were getting into supermarkets, stores, and the private label market. Everything was great until I started running into cash flow problems when Venezuela had some currency control problems that led to massive hyperinflation.

I had to do something drastic before I lost everything. One night, while washing my hands in a restaurant bathroom, I noticed that the soap dispensers had powdered soap. I thought, *Oh my gosh, this could be my big ah-ha moment. There is no soft soap in Venezuela.* I decided that we would be the first to offer soft soap in the country, and headed back to New York.

I found another $200,000 and took a bunch of soft soap samples back to Venezuela. I showed them to my chemical engineers and before I knew it, we were in the soft soap business. I also realized that not only was there no private label market, but the concept was unknown to them. I approached some of the country's larger distributors and offered them a private label using their name, so they could take ownership. They would help distribute my products across Venezuela and neighboring countries. They would take pride in doing so, because the products bore their name.

Business was good, and got better. Once, while on the veranda behind the warehouse, where we ate lunch and enjoyed cigars and cognac and the marvelous view of the hills, I realized I was truly playing the part. I had the cigars, the white suit and hat, and was definitely living in a dream. A few hours later, I got pulled over by a cop.

Cops in Venezuela were called the Death Patrol. They dressed in black and rode black motorcycles. My Spanish was not that good, but I knew enough to tell them I had to call my lawyer.

When I first got to Venezuela, Bernardo, my lawyer, assured me that if I ever had a problem, he could get me out of it, as long as I didn't end up at the police station. At that point it might be too late to come to my rescue. I explained the situation to Bernardo and handed the cell phone to the policeman. I could hear them talking in Spanish.

The policeman gave me the phone back and Bernardo instructed me to give my wallet to the cop, so I did. The cop looked at me, I looked at the cop, and he took everything from my wallet and handed it back to me empty. Once he had all my IDs and money, he took off on his motorcycle. This life-threatening situation made me realize that something was going on in this country. As I continued home, I noticed National Guard soldiers everywhere.

I thought, *There have been coups before — perhaps I am in the middle of one.* I got home and rushed to the TV. They were reporting something about the International Monetary Fund (IMF) and a huge currency devaluation. Gasoline prices were skyrocketing and there was blood in the streets. The next thing I knew, hyperinflation hit. When you live in a third-world country and experience 5% to 15% inflation month after month, it is hard to stay afloat.

The government tells you that you have to stamp a price (price controls) on your products and give your employees raises so they could afford to weather the economic storm.

Manufacturers like myself got nothing, however. Suppliers could order goods, hold them a few months, and sell them for 20% more, but I could not do the same. It was the beginning of the end for me in Venezuela.

I knew that one of my best friends, Roy, wanted to change his life, so I wrote to him. He was with an accounting firm in New York City, but his passion was entrepreneurship. He was helping me figure out how to liquidate my inventory and decided to fly down to Venezuela and change his life, perhaps as my CFO if he and I succeeded in turning around the company. We could storm the rest of South America together.

There was just one problem. No money was coming in. My debtors were not paying any of what they owed. I realized my business was just one of credit. All I did was receive and give credit. I would not get paid for 30, 60, 90, or 120 days. The country's economic and political situation was deteriorating, so fewer and fewer people paid their bills. One day, Roy picked up a handful of unpaid invoices from a supermarket down the block and said we would have to go there in person and get our $5,000.

The proprietor said he did not have it. Roy did not speak Spanish, but was determined to get $5,000 in value out of the guy. He nodded toward the liquor section and told me to grab two shopping carts. He told the guy, "We are not leaving empty handed, so we will fill up our two carts." That's exactly what we did. By the time I got back to my apartment, it was crystal clear to me that this game was over. I was not going to collect the money owed to me, and I needed to get out of there fast, before civil war broke out.

We packed our stuff and hid out on the coast for a month or so. We had eggs every morning, washed down with plenty of alcohol at breakfast, lunch, and dinner. As I started working on Plan B, Roy brought me two books: *Excel for Dummies* and *Stock Options for Dummies*. I will never forget reading the book on Excel. The left side of my brain said, *This isn't going to work and the only sell you're ever going to understand will be a jail cell if you don't get out of here.* The right side said, *Oh boy!* and just could not stop making jokes, like *Why don't we give the options book a try?* That's what I did, and I started envisioning a new future.

I decided to figure out what had gone wrong over the last few years before heading back to the states. I wanted to be a better person, to learn from failure, and perhaps go to work for a more established company to improve my skills. When I look back, I realize I was entirely too trusting.

I should have researched the country more before I went there, and I should have left earlier. Whoever said, "Hang in there until the very end" was incorrect. I should have called it quits months before I ran out of money. I cost my investors and friends a lot of money. Now I had to start over and explain to everyone what went wrong.

I moved back to New York and entered a stock trading program. I passed a few tests (7 and 63), and all the exams. I was ready for a new life, but it was hard to not only not be the boss, but to have to start again at the very bottom.

I lost my mother and I was just completely thrown out of my rhythm in life. I was in a mourning period and I wanted to get back to that happy period, so I decided to go back to San Francisco, because that was my hometown and my college town.

I went back to San Francisco. I found my girlfriend, and the next thing I knew I was in this sadistic, military stock trading program. I clocked in at 4 a.m. every day, and I had to make 1,000 cold calls to people across the country; I was nothing but a glorified phone connector, trying to determine if people were qualified to invest with the firm. If you did not hit your goals in the afternoon, you had to stay to call Europe. If you did not hit your goals that night, you had to stay to call Australia. If you did not hit your goals by then, you had to call Asia. You had to stay, stay, stay.

I stayed for almost a year, dialing that phone more than 300,000 times. There was no cheating. If you had a hard time reaching your goals, you had to call more and more people. I finally got a break, that Valentine's Day, when I heard from Jason, an old friend. He apologized for not getting back with me when I had called him months or years earlier, asking for advice. He was going through problems of his own, just as I was. He said, "Hey, I've got this opportunity: a floor in downtown New York City in the Merck. It's a commodity trading business. And we just expanded, so I'm living in Texas."

Jason explained that he was part of a natural gas business that was absolutely unbelievable. He said there was a pre-paid plane ticket waiting for me at the San Francisco airport that would take me to Cancun. He would introduce to me to some people he was working with in Mexico. "Your flight leaves in a few hours," he said.

A million thoughts buzzed through my head. At the time the flight was set to depart, my girlfriend had planned to be at my house on Haight Street, with a special Valentine's Day dinner. She made me promise that I would be there, and not get distracted by the next big idea. Yet this huge idea had just dropped into my lap.

I talked to her and ended up going to Cancun. Jason was right. I met all these traders and brokers, and it was so exciting. It was like Venezuela, but bigger. I never knew you could spend $10,000 on a single meal until that trip. I also found out you could go the jewelry store in the Ritz-Carlton and spend $40,000 on a watch. Each trader I met behaved like this. They worked in what was known as derivative markets. Jason did futures and contracts. All of it was a mystery to me, but it was exciting to watch all the pit traders on TV, yelling and screaming. I heard that people become very wealthy overnight, and I wanted to be part of it.

A new opportunity, called Electricity Contracts, was on the horizon. All the markets in the United States were going to be deregulated, which would open up a huge opportunity for me to get involved in an entry-level position on the ground floor. Back in San Francisco, I got an offer from the company in Texas. They would pay me a whopping $24,000 a year, a $2,000 a month base salary. That was more than I made in San Francisco in my brutal job as a stockbroker phoning 300,000 people who never wanted to hear from me in the first place.

My girlfriend was not happy, so I decided that was a good time to get engaged, so she could feel like she was part of my future and help me grow mine, as well. She said yes, and then I told about moving to Texas. We moved, and I started in a clerical position that was humbling, yet not so humbling. There were pits of people yelling and screaming numbers in the room. My job was to write them down as fast as I could on a board so the brokers in the room could report them to their traders and help transact trades.

I worked with my back turned to all those people in the relentless, overwhelming chaos, and it was rough. They threw stuff at me when impatient or upset. They yelled when I didn't write down the numbers fast enough. It was not a glorious period in my life, but I realized I needed to learn the business inside and out from someone else's point of view. I knew what went wrong in my first venture, and I wanted to learn everything correctly, from the ground up, to be prepared for my next venture.

I got my shot about six months later, when they moved me to a spot desk in an area called West Coast Power. I couldn't be part of the more lucrative, 10-year deals, because I was in a 24-hour business where you were paid for a single day's work, instead of the ten-year calendar product which would be getting paid for 3650 days. All I had to do was call a bunch of utility traders and introduce myself and my services. This was easy for me, coming from the stock brokering business.

One time, one of my utility customers invited my wife and me out to the balloon festival in Albuquerque, New Mexico, a spectacular event when a few thousand hot air balloons are aloft at the same time.

I was with my wife and colleagues in the air, among the other balloons, and we were feeling serene and peaceful. Without warning, huge gusts of wind kicked in and before we knew what was going on, our balloon was out of control. The pilot yanked on the cord, trying to get above the stream of air. He failed, and we were thrown around and headed straight into a building, in a life-threatening situation.

We smacked into the roof. The basket knocked out air conditioner units as it scraped along. We tumbled on top of each other, unable to see clearly. It was one of the most frightening moments of my life. We finally cleared the building and set sail again, unable to control our flight. We held on for a few hours, but never regained control. The pilot began a crash landing near an airport, and just before we collided with some power lines, he was miraculously able to duck below them to land.

Once we verified that everyone was safe, someone asked me how things were going in Texas. I replied that I was not making much money, and my wife and I drove cars with no air conditioning in the super humid, 100-degree Houston summers. He said, "Next week, you will get a call from somebody in New York City. I suggest you take it and fly up to meet with them. They will offer you a job."

The call came from a company called Bloomberg. They wanted to take everything I did in the pits and put it on an electronic trading screen for my customers to use. I was not sure how I was going to get that done, but I gave my standard reply: "I will get it done, easy."

I said, "The city is expensive. What can you pay me?"

They said, "Well, Alan, what do you make now?"

That caught me off guard, and all I could think to say was, "$124,000." I put $100,000 in front of my current $24,000. I said, "I cannot afford to live in the city." They looked at me and said, "You know what? We will make you a onetime offer of $175,000." I said, "You know what? This sounds like a very interesting opportunity. I'll take it. "

I flew home and told my wife we were moving to New York. I worked for that company for a few years, learning and growing and having a blast. They invested in their employees, teaching me a lot about business and life. I decided I would be a lifer there, but as so often is the case, just when you get comfortable, opportunity comes knocking.

Another company offered me twice my salary, at $350K — it was pre-IPO, and they also promised stock options and warrants. They needed me to build something for them, something I did well for another company. Still, I didn't want to go.

I told Bloomberg what I was worth in the market, and when they offered me a paltry 5% raise, I knew I had to go. I couldn't turn down the opportunity to make $1 million in the next 12 months, with a two-year commitment. I had to walk away. I also told the new company, "Let me bring one of my partners in, as well," and the two of us went to this new company, a well-known startup with a great track record in the industry.

They were supposed to release some software, but were behind schedule. When the launch day came, the software was not ready. Forty of us were schedule to go out and mend fences, but 38 people canceled, leaving just Stu and me to set things right

Stu said, "You know what? Let's go do this." On the way out, my partner was pulled back by the CEO, and I was the only one headed to the West Coast.

I left on September 10, 2001, taking the elevator down from the 101st floor of the World Trade Center. I got in the car, went to the airport, and flew to Portland to meet with representatives from Enron. I woke up 12 hours later to my cell phone ringing, then saw that 700 out of the 1,000 people in my company had been killed in the top five floors of the World Trade Center's North Tower. I lost 40 out of 44 teammates that day. All I could do was sit on the bed in this nondescript hotel room in Portland, with a TV my only connection to the world.

As a manager, I tried desperately to reach others. I called spouses and parents. I learned that the CEO, CFO, a drunk clerk who overslept, and I were the only survivors from our division. I spent a week all alone in my hotel room in Portland. Once I got past the mourning, I started to focus on my future after being wiped out yet again. My opportunity to make $1 million per year was gone, never to return. But that wasn't the most important loss. Forget the warrants, forget the stock — forget all that stuff. Before, I could stand in the backyard of my condo and look at the World Trade Center. I chose that home because I could live a few blocks away from the World Trade Center.

The train carried me under the river to work there every day. Now, all of it was gone.

I changed my life that week. I decided to be more than just a businessman, chasing money. From that point on, I would be interested in everyone I encountered. I would be a real entrepreneur. At some point along the way, I got lost, and I needed to get back to my roots. I gave five years of my life to others, and I had nothing to show for it. No brand, no nothing.

I realized that if I had my own businesses, or asset, or brand, I would rebuild quicker. That was not the case, and I was afraid.

I will never forget the time when I hired this kid, Dougie, out of a bar in Hoboken. He was a bar back, and he was always excited to see us walk into the bar around 4 p.m. or 5 p.m. Monday through Friday. I can always tell when somebody wants a job. Their eyes light up and they will do whatever it takes. He had that whatever-it-takes attitude, so I gave him an opportunity.

Dougie was young, about 21. He was working in the World Trade Center that day, in my seat, and I remember speaking with his family. His father was a steel worker on the New Jersey side and he was building a tower. He saw all these attacks happen from the 55th floor. I could only imagine how horrified he felt.

I went back to New Jersey, and the company told me I had to go to Houston. My wife and I moved to the suburb of Pearland, and less than three months later, I got fired when the company closed. I actually had a contract, but I still got fired. This was when I set up my new house office, with 18 lines, to sell hourly power. This set me on the course towards my first single-family house.

CHAPTER 6

# Single-Family Houses

Sometimes in life, we find a method that works so well that we just want to jump up, scream for joy, and shout to the rest of the world. Some people call that religion. Others just have a single a-ha breakthrough. For me, the method was with single-family houses.

I played a game when I was young that involved connecting dots to make as many squares as possible. My new venture was like this game, and I called it "Five Steps to an Eight-Digit Net Worth" — (1) buy cheap, (2) fix, (3) rent, (4) refi, and (5) hold — and it is my favorite game. You don't have to be a genius to play; I taught my 12-year-old son how to do it. Passion is more important than brainpower. I created simple formulas and systems that worked well for my entire team. I did the same thing every time, for many years.

It was beautiful, sitting in my cubicle while working full time in corporate America and accessing satellite images of houses sent to me via Internet email. I used the Internet to run comps and rent comps. All the while, I sent my team marching orders via text messages.

I found a good broker and contractor. I learned how to work with a virtual assistant, one who lived in Europe. She would get most of the work done while we slept, and handled a few more details throughout the day since she suffered from insomnia. I was able to buy many houses.

I got much more for the houses than I was paying, and it was very exciting. Some of the houses that I bought had profit of $50 up to $300 or $400 a month. I was finally able to escape the airtight, sealed submarine of corporate America.

Each time I profited from a house, I was one step closer to retirement, to the fulfillment of my dreams, and to having enough time to do what I wanted in life. A few years after I bought my first house, my wife and I were financially free. It was because of the Cash Flow Mindset: I was creating a personal ATM machine. But our sense of freedom wasn't just from collecting profit after our expenses were paid; it was about feeling comfortable with our decisions to move on to a new place in our lives. Being able to ask myself if I wanted to continue working in corporate America was a huge milestone. I could leave.

It's funny now, looking back at the hours I spent in traffic driving home from work. Every day, I literally created millions of dollars of equity while on my cell phone. The longer I was stuck in the car, the more money I made, and the more wheeling and dealing and finding houses I did. When I was on the phone, I felt like I had one job in life, which was to get the other side to say, "Yes."

With a few hundred dollars and a loan, we found our first investment house in Alvin, Texas. We brought this house in for $23,000. The budget for repairs and rehab was $7,000. We were in this investment for less than $30,000. This one house started my own real estate empire. I will never forget how proud we were. We turned the ugliest house on the street into a tiny kingdom. Our first rental house was one that anyone would be proud to call home. Each month, we made hundreds of dollars in profit. It snowballed. It got bigger, and bigger, and bigger while we bought more properties. The definition of wealth was becoming clearer to me: it was all about having money work for you.

The house appraised for $75,000. Like any good real estate entrepreneur-investor, we refinanced. We pulled out the original investment, paid back the first lender, then found a new lender. We also pulled out some extra money on the deal by bringing the house up to the same value as the others on the street. When a house is run down and unwanted, people become blind to its real value. Here lies the real opportunity in fixing up property for others: forcing the equity.

By cleaning up and repairing the property, we increased its value to match that of other homes in the area. We always targeted $25,000 of forced equity into the deal or we wouldn't bother. We would borrow the funds, so we had no money of our own involved in many of our deals. After refinancing, we used the extra money to buy the next house so we didn't have to borrow as much. We did this routinely and consistently for years while we built multiple businesses.

One trick in life is having profits exceed expenses. I found that if you have less pressure to perform during your corporate job "servitude," the more freedom you have and the more chances you will be willing to take on yourself and any new ventures. I found myself taking more calculated risks because I had more free time to allocate to figuring out and studying new investments.

I clearly focused on my future and building my legacy with cash-flowing assets — a legacy bank for my family. I built my energy brokerage shop while buying single-family houses. The leverage with both of these was tremendous, but I found myself in corporate America owning a very risky business. Occasionally, we found ourselves trying to steal market shares away from bigger competitors — and by bigger,

I mean billion-dollar cap, publicly traded companies that didn't think twice about slapping lawsuits on all kinds of frivolous situations when we found ourselves in court. Usually, when a small company opposes a large company, settlements happen very quickly. Both parties agree to agree on a negotiation.

The knowledge that I had cash flow from the houses gave me extra confidence to stare down my competitors. In a negotiation, or a court situation or mediation — where perhaps they felt like I was one step closer to closing my doors because I could not afford to fight them (although they were very wrong if they thought this) — my opponent did not know that I had the cash flow behind me from my houses and real estate investments to keep the doors open on my other investments, too. I learned through this business that it can sometimes be better to be patient than to just write a check, in real estate or any business transaction.

While all my businesses were running relatively smoothly, I found good brokers. Every Sunday night we put in bids on a computer system to buy government foreclosures. Monday morning, Michael, the broker, let me know if I got the deal or not. A few weeks later, if I did get the deal, the closer would come to me, because I could not leave my office. My virtual assistant set up all the needed activities once I bought the house, including the process of working with the general contractor via telephone. We set a system up with the general contractor, which worked out very well for us.

We asked the general contractor to choose from three options in fixing these houses:

A.  $5,000 a month in rehab.

B.  $10,000 a month in rehab.

C.  $15,000 for the house and no more no less.

No overages and no unders. If they said $10,000, they chose Option B for $10,000, whether they finished on time or not. This system was efficient and prevented bad situations. I see so many people get involved in disagreements with their general contractors. Our approach allowed us to buy one house a month for about ten years, about 120 houses. Under our approach, I could force equity appreciation.

I have a saying: "Everyone needs a house. Everyone needs a safe place to go." I was very confident in buying as many single-family houses as I could afford. I quickly came to understand how much the land (the dirt itself) cost, and what it cost to build houses. I found myself buying houses 20 to 40 cents on the dollar. My money was always working for us, looking for a good deal. If it found a great deal, a sense of urgency propelled us to move quickly. If not, patience and persistence always got the job done.

I had a formula. Every time I bought a small rent house, there would be at least $25,000 of equity left over in the deal. For example, when I bought that first house for $23,000 and fixed it up for $7,000, I was in the deal for $30,000. That particular deal appraised for $75,000, minus closing costs. I made a profit with $30,000 in just one house. My goal was to purchase 12 houses per year while I worked full time in corporate America. In doing so, with the minimum of $25,000 a month in equity per deal, I increased my balance sheet and net worth by $300,000 a year.

As I got more comfortable with the monthly cash flows from my houses, I discovered yet another strategy, which I call mini-units and define as $25,000. These chunks of cash came from house flips and were used for down payments for more assets.

Occasionally, I used them to pay for a vacation, such as when I sold a house for $25,135.13 profit, more than enough to pay for a vacation for three to Okinawa. The day I arrived, I was excited to log into my computer and check my updated bank balance. To my surprise, there amounted wired was $251,351.30. The title company had put the comma in the wrong place! It was hilarious to say the least. I never had so much money in my checking account.

Halfway through the trip, the bank called me to send back the funds. I explained that I would not be wiring funds in the middle of the Pacific, 6,000 miles from home, but would send the cash when I returned. They weren't too happy, but understood.

## The Three Steps of Single-Family Houses

I'm sure you can see how these kinds of transactions can vastly affect your net worth, balance sheet, and ability to borrow money, and can create an incredible future for you and your family. As I kept buying houses, the cash flows kept snowballing, growing bigger and bigger.

After a while, I stopped thinking about the Cash Flow Mindset. It was turning into a philosophy, an assumed way of life. I will never forget the moment I became financially free, when the cash flow and profits from my rental properties were significantly more than my expenses. I asked myself:

*Do I want to continue working? Do I like how I'm spending my time and other resources, or would I like using them somewhere else instead?*

Over the years, I captured millions of dollars in equity. I refinanced a lot of that money, pulling a lot of it out of real estate deals. It's comparable to being at a casino or trading stocks, because the money is not yours until you cash out and leave. Today, my portfolio involves hundreds of single-family houses, and thousands of apartment units. I have no money in any of those deals. I was capturing millions of dollars of equity and cashing out my money.

I bought countless houses that cost $30,000 to $40,000, and spent an average of $10,000 fixing them up. Most appraised for over $90,000. By refinancing, I had plenty of opportunity to pull out all my cash and move it into the next group of houses, to repeat the cash flow process. To this day, I still refinance these houses to either pull out tax-free, spendable money or reinvest in other assets.

It is a three-step dance: (1) buy a house for $40,000, (2) spend $10,000 to fix it up, and (3) get a bank to give me back all my money. My balance sheet reflected at least a $25,000 gain in net worth. Do the math. It wasn't long before the houses were worth over a net position of $2.5 million on over $10 million of real estate, without investing a penny of my own funds!

Take advantage of your opportunities, because one thing leads to another. When you can put that on your profit and loss statement, balance sheet, and cash flow statements, well now . . . I call this the banker's game. Banks consider your money a liability, and your house to be their asset. In my three-step dance, I made the moves that a banker makes and thought how they think. Every time I bought one of those houses, I used that equity to pump up my balance sheet to make it look like I was bigger than I actually was — which is the way it works.

My profits grew. I was increasing my cash flow and becoming my own ATM machine. This was my mantra when things got tough. I often stared at this simple chart to keep me focused on my dream of 100 houses and make it through the day.

| | | |
|---|---|---|
| ☐ | Paid | $40,000 |
| ☐ | Rehab | $10,000 |
| ☐ | Refi | $50,000 |
| | Balance Sheet Profit: | $25,000 |

In life, if you can leave something better than you found it, you can make money. Everything I bought was broken and needed to be fixed. This turned out to be the theme of my real estate career. I followed this quick formula to wealth, learning more along the way.

The routine of buying the same product catches up with you when there either isn't enough supply or there is too much demand. When that happens, you are forced to take more risk. I upped my numbers and started running more projects simultaneously.

| | | |
|---|---|---|
| ☐ | Paid | $60,000 |
| ☐ | Rehab | $15,000 |
| ☐ | Refi | $75,000 |

Balance Sheet Profit:   $50,000

When I couldn't find deals that had enough captured profit, I decided to start building my own houses to manufacture my own profits. Once I bought a large piece of land for $30,000, subdivided it into three lots, and built three houses.

| | | |
|---|---|---|
| ☐ | Paid | $30,000 |
| ☐ | Cost to Build | $270,000 |
| ☐ | Refi | $300,000 |

Balance Sheet Profit:   $90,000

## Five Businesses for Cash flow

To keep busy, if I couldn't buy cheap, used houses, I built new ones. In the single-family house business, there are multiple ways to make money and increase your ability to constantly do so.

1.  Buy land and build houses
2.  Buy cheap houses and fix them
3.  Lend money to others to do the same
4.  Flip retail/cheap houses
5.  Teach others how to do this

I always have five businesses running. Some are busier than others. It depends on the time of year and what I want do. The bottom line is to always keep busy and generate money. It is possible to have all five feeding off each other and profiting from each business as it functions as a whole. Let me give you an example.

I built a house and sold it. I made $60,000 from the sale, and rolled it into the purchase of a cheap house for $50,000, and I spent $10,000 fixing it. I sold the house for $110,000 and paid the closing fees. I walked away with $100,000 and took an eight-week sabbatical.

Before I left, I lent $100,000 to a student who paid me $50,000 to teach him everything I know about real estate and to become partners. I lent the money under the condition that I would receive 1% a month in interest and we would split the profit from the sale of the student's first home. The house sold 120 days later, and I made $4,000 in interest and $10,000.

| | |
|---|---|
| Buy and Build | $60,000 |
| Buy and Fix | $40,000 |
| Lend | $50,000 |
| Flip | $4,000 |
| Teach/Mentor          + | $10,000 |

Total profit:     $164,000

It's up to you to decide how much time you want to spend in each category. I've seen people build multi-million-dollar educational companies on this system. Some start off as real estate entrepreneurs and end up falling in love with the education process. Others believe they can make more looking for deals. It's up to you.

Personally, I've fallen in love with the complete system. I let the market dictate what's hot and what's not. If I can't find houses, I'll spend more time lending, educating, and partnering. When the pendulum swings and I find too many houses, I'll spend less time lending and teaching. Each of the five businesses can explode into growth and other businesses. I've seen others who started off in real estate and ended up migrating into completely unrelated ventures, such as internet marketing and website creation.

When I had my first child, I bought a house in Windsor. Not exactly Windsor Castle in a far-off, romantic destination, but the Windsor that is a blue-collar, working neighborhood in Texas. I didn't have a lot of rental houses at the time, but my plan was to allocate a house for my first child and pay for his education. Let's take a look at the numbers 13 years later.

| | | |
|---|---|---|
| ☐ | Paid | $30,000 |
| ☐ | Rehab | $10,000 |
| ☐ | Refi | $40,000 |

Balance Sheet Profit:   $100,000

This house makes $150 a month and pays down the $40,000 mortgage by $75 a month. Let's look at the numbers again:

| | | |
|---|---|---|
| Profits: | | $1,800 a year |
| Pays down the mortgage: | | $900 a year |
| Potential opportunity to pay: | | $2,700 a year |
| ☐ | Paid | $30,000 |
| ☐ | Rehab | $10,000 |
| ☐ | Refi | $40,000 |
| ☐ | Balance | $4,900 |
| ☐ | Market Value | $140,000 |

Balance Sheet Profit:   $135,000

I have no money in the deal. By using the strategy of buying cheap, fixing up and renting, and refinancing the tenant, this deal is paying for my son's education. In a few years, we will own the house outright. There's a great chance that this one house — out of the hundreds in my portfolio — will pay for my son's tuition and more.

## Big Uncle A

I expanded on this model in helping family members. I have a handful of siblings and nieces and nephews and receive requests for money, loans, and college tuition assistance. Here is the example of how I was Big Uncle A in Project Nephew.

I decided to take matters into my own hands and combine all the classes, seminars, and courses I created over the years into a new program that touches on the cash flow philosophy, its associated responsibilities, and the multi-millionaire mentality. I included information from the best weekend retreats I attended. Much of this information is found in this book.

I had my nephew move to Texas and met him for one hour every Monday morning. My lessons were well organized. We started with the basic understanding of money management, and tips and tricks to warp-speed the passage of time. We proceeded to the single-family home business, and all that homes in disrepair offer. In less than two years, he had well over six figures in the bank, as well as multiple businesses.

In accordance with life's principles, he also teaches what he wants to better understand. He is right on my heels, eyeing commercial real estate. Most importantly, he's asking the right questions, and realizing that his potential is bigger than he can ever imagine.

## Get Uncomfortable

(*trust your process*)

Entering the apartment business forced me to step out of my comfort zone and create business systems that went beyond what I was comfortable doing. This helped me build the Cash Flow Mindset I was already working on, but forced me to make the numbers bigger and create new business systems.

When I found that first, 76-unit apartment building via the Internet (discussed in Chapter 2), the broker told me that the seller would owner-finance it. At the time, I didn't understand what that meant, but I got the gist: I could buy a $2 million asset with a $40,000 down payment, and that worked very well for me. I was very excited.

On the way home from Tokyo to close on the deal four weeks later, I knew I was starting a new chapter in my life. I knew that the apartment building process is very much like running a small business. You have accounting, HR, and managers. Your customers are your tenants, and you have lenders. It was an eye-opener that changed the game for me.

Once your systems are running on automatic and everyone is doing what they are supposed to be doing, you start trusting the process. You see how everybody interacts with each other and stop trying to be a jack-of-all-trades who thinks he can do every single job.

The jack-of-all-trades mentality keeps others from applying their expertise and skills. When you realize this, the world of business opens up for you. I got a glimpse of this while running my first apartment building. After putting the systems and processes (and my knowledge) in place as part of the day-to-day operation, the sky was the limit. My purchases got bigger and bigger, and so, too, did my cash flow. All of this improved my lifestyle tremendously.

CHAPTER 7

# Multi-Family Housing

I found that the ideas I learned from investing in multi-family housing taught me how to think in bigger and wiser terms. This process enforced the need to be a lifelong learner. I was always looking to improve in my quest for new ideas by reading, and attending seminars. I was fully engaged in fulfilling the number-one desire in humans to expand whatever we are involved in.

Multi-family housing taught me how each apartment complex is a business, an island unto itself. An aspect that I love is that we get to try new things and move into different arenas by applying the same rules of the game. Ultimately, we create value or we do not; we make a profit or we do not; we fill our buildings with tenants or we do not. Reinvention exists so that we can continue to grow. Success is growth, and I'm a big believer in improving 1% a day. If you can do this to your bottom line numbers, the rewards will be unbelievable.

## Debt Is the New Money

Managing debt and understanding how the world of money works blew open another door of understanding for me. If banks pay less than 1% in interest to their depositors and lend at 4%, that's a three-point difference, or spread. Factor in the rate of inflation, and it is clearly impossible for the average person to get ahead without leveraging real estate and business. I used debt to stay ahead of inflation.

My plan was to borrow as much as I could and hold on to it for as long as I could. If the cost of a single piece of wood or a brick increases over the next 10 years, I win. If I came across an apartment building that was on sale for half price, I considered that a winning formula on steroids. The bank would lend me 70% and my investors would bring the other 30%. Other times, I used debt to get my money out of a deal without paying taxes or selling the asset. At this point, when you get all your money out of the deal, your returns and profits are infinite. With this strategy, you can do as many deals as you like.

I think back to the day when I was afraid to look past single-family houses but learned that cycles, economies, and personal tastes will change. My education and ability seemed to be reaching full potential — after all, I had bought 300 houses — and I was looking for a new, fresh, invigorating, and exciting challenge. It seemed normal in my life to change directions every three to five years. I always looked for changes and needed to make changes within my investment psychology.

Chasing rent money never works. If the tenant or customer didn't pay, we'd move them out as fast as possible and work on being more selective the next time. In other words, it was a numbers game. When I could not find enough houses to buy, I was forced to go beyond my comfort level, and was suddenly confronted with the magnitude of buying multi-family housing to speed up the wealth process. I constantly reminded myself to not think average, but to think *massive*.

In real estate, you quickly start to understand that the less money you have in a deal, the higher rate of return on your investment.

There was a time when I had a million dollars in a deal and turned it into seven million, and best of all, no money came out of my pocket. Partners contributed the financing and I contributed my skills and abilities. I was smart enough to fix the problem, to leverage my dimes into dollars! This process became the mechanism that sped it all up, allowing me to buy real estate that was beyond the reach of most individuals, but this journey began with a simple, 76-unit building. You can't buy an apartment building until you know how to use debt. When you understand the process, you can buy as many as you want! I quickly learned that money is debt and all I needed was financial education on the process. My personal projections consisted of how much cheap debt I could accumulate.

## Buying a House versus an Apartment Complex

*(it takes the same amount of time...)*

It became obvious that it takes as much time and planning to buy one house as it does to buy a 76-unit apartment complex. I was amazed when I realized this, and after that, there was no turning back. I shot for the moon, ready to catch a star.

I bought my first apartment complex without any partners or investors. I just picked up the phone and called the broker while I was in Japan to ask about an Internet listing of his. It was like chasing a phantom through the fog. I didn't get many responses until the day a broker named Scott called me. He told me that it was incredible timing — and incredible luck — because this particular deal had just fallen out of contract. The owner was desperate to get rid of it.

The seller was a cosmetic dentist who decided to make a career change, then changed his mind. Once he got involved in the apartment business, he realized how much he loved being a dentist. He was willing to owner finance the complex, meaning my $40,000 down payment would give me control over a $1.7 million asset, with the possibility of cash flowing $5,000 a month.

With the help of my team, I learned many different ways to profit from this debt. Most of us are taught to avoid debt, but if it weren't for this first venture, I never would have learned how to harness $100 million of debt for my benefit.

First, as time goes by each month, part of the payments made reduce your debt while simultaneously increasing your net worth. I always considered that a forced savings account. There are also huge interest tax write-off advantages.

Debt allows you to use financial leverage in ways that you could never imagine. When combined, these methods offer legal ways to not pay taxes on earned income that crosses valid real estate deductions and losses. The next question was the following: How many more times do I need to do that before I can be absolutely financially free and develop massive net worth?

All I had to do was raise the rents and decrease the expenses while improving the business. These numbers were vastly exploited when I could save a dime, because each time I did, I would make 10 times my money back. This is a simple idea. You want to be in any business where you create 10 times your money — you're literally bending over to pick up the dimes to make dollars.

With this owner-financed deal, I didn't need to apply for a new loan, so we could speed up the closing and take ownership within a few weeks. It was a very exciting time for me because all I needed was that down payment.

I ended up buying the apartment complex from the dentist and running it. Everything worked out perfectly. I liked the area and bought more properties in addition to the many single-family homes

I owned there. I could turn the leasing office of one of my apartment complexes into a leasing office for the houses, as well.

| ☐ | Paid | $1.7 million |
|---|------|--------------|
| ☐ | Rehab | $50,000 |
| ☐ | Sold | $2.1 million |
| | | Profit: $350,000 |

My next venture was into the world of distressed properties: taking back bank-owned property, otherwise known as REO foreclosed real estate. My first transaction of this type was like being in a horror movie, going to the dark side, where you can put all your eggs into one non-refundable deposit, after which you will learn what's behind door number one, two, and three, *if* the bank chooses to sign your letter of intent, that is.

My next purchase was a 34-unit building that was in great shape and, believe it or not, at $450,000, was half the price of the one I had just paid for up the street.

A few years later, I sold the property for $1 million. This experience was a huge eye-opener for me. I began to understand how to use debt and leverage to get into bigger properties. Borrowing money on this deal was actually easier than buying a few small rental houses. It over-appraised, so I was able to pull my money out with an additional $250,000 for my next apartment complex purchase.

| ☐ | Paid | $450,000 |
|---|------|----------|
| ☐ | Rehab | $50,000 |
| ☐ | Sold | $1.1 million |
| | | Profit: $600,000 |

# One Apartment Complex Can Change Your Life

Since I knew it was possible to buy a house at a 50% discount, I decided to look for apartments at a half-off discount. Sometimes in life, you need to bet on your strengths, and I have always found good deals. As the economy faltered, prices fell and I ended up buying another apartment complex. I applied the psychology I learned in the commodity markets, which we called averaging down. On my first purchase, up the block, I paid $25,000 per apartment unit. Now, I paid $12,500.

We were clearly in a falling market. I needed to adjust quickly, maneuver faster, and buy as many as I could afford. It seemed like everyone was looking for the exit, which was a "buy" signal for me, because I had seen similar situations in the stock and commodities markets. When there are sellers but no buyers, things can quickly get ugly — few people can create order out of chaos, but that is exactly what this situation required.

One mile down the road was a 52-unit building that was more difficult to purchase, because the roof had never been repaired properly after a hurricane, and it still had tenants. The day I bought it, the city sent a task force that took over my complex and relocated every single tenant. It was very depressing to watch my tenants and cash flow being driven away in a beautiful, brand-new bus. I ended up with an empty apartment complex.

|  |  |  |
|---|---|---|
| ☐ | Paid | $300,000 |
| ☐ | Rehab | $500,000 |
| ☐ | Sold | $1.2 million |
|  | Profit: | $400,000 |

If you think the story gets any easier for me, you are very wrong. I needed more pain and a bigger challenge. This motivated me to purchase a 160-unit foreclosure. I was tired of simply talking about ideas like so many others; I wanted to execute them, as well. I chose not just any foreclosure but a boarded up, bank-owned REO, patrolled by guards and occasionally helicopter flyovers, in one of the worst parts of town.

When I buy any property, I look for an advantage, and one of the things that attracted me was its location across the street from a school. Sounds like a great idea, right? Well, after I purchased this complex, I learned that it required serious rehab. As I always do, I asked myself a question: What is the one thing I can do to make an improvement here? The law of diminishing effect works in my favor. For example, I can replace an overgrown field with a new playground. I can apply a fresh coat of paint to the exterior of the entire complex. This complex was large, on five acres, so I decided to open it in phases.

What I call the dark spiral began soon after that. A few drive-by shootings near my general contractors definitely slowed down progress in phase one. Helicopter chases were common in the area, and one day, a driver exited the highway and came to a stop in my parking lot. The driver did not live there, but his girlfriend did. He got out of the car, run up the stairs, and barricaded himself in one of my apartment units.

Homeland Security showed up regularly, looking for bank robbers. It's never good when folks show up in black cars and black uniforms. I will never forget the time my maintenance man unclogged a sewage back up and pulled wads of hundred-dollar bills from the pipes. That, my friends, is what Homeland Security was looking for.

And to cap things off, by the time phase two was ready to open, the school across the street closed.

This was a very exciting time, and yielded <u>fantastic profit</u>.

| | | |
|---|---|---|
| ☐ | Paid | $700,000 |
| ☐ | Rehab | $1.7 million+ |
| ☐ | Sold | $2.6 million |
| | | Profit: (… very little) |

Another time, during a real estate seminar, the speaker showed us a photo of an apartment complex I had bought four weeks prior. Unbeknownst to me, the building was closed because of a bat infestation. Apparently, bats excrete dangerous chemicals. The city required the poor soul who owned it before me, Buyer A, to "strip it down to the studs" by tearing out all the sheetrock and wiring, then condemned it.

This put Buyer A out of business and the building went back to the bank. In comes Buyer B, who requested a new loan and did an amazing job fixing up the complex with new countertops, new washers and dryers, new flooring, new roofing, and new wiring. Unfortunately, the bank demanded the money back prematurely because of the financial crisis. In comes buyer C which is me.

By the time I closed this deal, the company checking account $82, and I was on my way to Florida. I paid $1.1 million and it immediately appraised for $2.25 million, then for $4 million the next year and for $6.5 million four years later. I wish I could say that the profit was all mine, but I had to share it with a partner. We refinanced and made an absolute fortune while having no money of our own tied up in the deal. These are my favorite kinds of deals.

I have a saying that one apartment complex can change your life. This one certainly did, eventually paying out north of $25,000 a month in cash flow/profit for a very, very long time. My monthly distribution (half of the income) was $12,5000 a month that arrived like clockwork and paid for my new, multi-million-dollar house. Completing this deal took me no more than 10 hours because I had an excellent property management company overseeing it. I must admit, I only went there once or twice a year. I still manage the financials online.

| | | |
|---|---|---|
| ☐ | Paid | $1.125 million |
| ☐ | Rehab | $750,000 |
| ☐ | Appraisal | $6.2 million |
| ☐ | Equity | $4.325 million |

Other times, I will do quick apartment flips for chunks of cash that I can use for down payments on other properties. Occasionally, you will find yourself in a situation where you need 20% or 30% down. This is not usually the case, though. Quite a few sales are owner-financed and you can get in "very light," as we say in the business. I purchased a 65- unit building, added new carpet, tile, and paint and flipped it for a $300,000 profit within nine months.

## International Opportunities

The following is a great example of how I turned around a government foreclosure using a number of different processes to drive up profits by fixing problems and buying the property across   the street with no more money out of my pocket in a "no money down deal." I purchased a 136-unit apartment complex and expanded it to 286 units by merging two apartment complexes.

I found the building through a broker. It was in receivership, which occurs when an apartment complex is given back to the bank after the former owner no longer wants it, or loses it due to bad operations, management, or economic circumstances. The U.S. government guarantees the debt and ends up with these properties when things turn bad.

This next transaction earned the famous moniker, <u>The Bangkok Close</u>. I bought a property for $3 million. I raised approximately

$800,000 from my equity partners, and the bank made up the rest with a rehab involving lots of repositioning, paint, and flooring.

When I finally took control of the property, I learned it had 50 more vacant units, which the former management company failed to tell me prior to my purchase. With the help of my management team, we cut expenses and raised the income. We installed refrigerators and carpet where needed. I also replaced all the roofs and resurfaced the parking lots, which enabled us to charge for reserved parking. A year and a half later, the building appraised for over $6 million. I did all the proper repairs, turned it around successfully, and it remained fully occupied. In other words, I found something broken and fixed it.

Making a $3 million profit on an $800,000 investment made my partners very happy with me. I then convinced Goldman Sachs to be the lender on a complex across the street that I wanted to buy with no money down, using the first building as collateral in a process called cross-collateralization; that is, when you can take Property A to buy Property B and then the bank controls Property A and B as the lender.

The second building cost me $4 million. Again, I fixed the things that were broken. The tenants were happy and didn't mind paying a little more for the improvements, and the higher rents reduced my expenses.

When my remodeling job was finished, it was time for me to take my annual summer trip to Asia: my worldly hike. Before leaving, I met with my broker, Jeff. I was short on time, but have always made it a habit to meet with others who can represent me while I travel or build another business. I told him that if he found the right buyer, I would sell. And sure enough, he found buyers who needed to close fast. They were in the middle of an IRS 1031 Exchange, which allows investors to roll their profits into new deals and defer taxes, but there are many deadlines to meet. Their team flew out to the American Embassy (because I was out of the country and we had documents to notarize), and from there I sold the entire apartment complex for $14.2 million.

This was not the first time I closed a transaction internationally; it can be done from anywhere in the world. Needless to say, that night I had fun celebrating the Bangkok Close.

| | | |
|---|---|---|
| ☐ | Paid | $7 million |
| ☐ | Sold | $14 million |

Profit:  $6 million (after closing costs)

In one case, I paid $600,000 for a 68-unit apartment complex on a very popular highway. I ran the deal without putting too much into it. It always stayed full, and I sold it approximately two years later on an owner-financed deal. This one is very interesting because an international group put $600,000 down as a down payment, and I then created a note for $1 million. I took their $600,000 and paid off the bank, and had an attorney draw up a note making me the lender — and first position at that — for $1 million. I created a $1 million note out of thin air!

| | | |
|---|---|---|
| ☐ | Paid | $550,000 |
| ☐ | Rehab | $50,000 |
| ☐ | Sold | $1.6 million |

Profit: $1 million Note

## Auctions and Non-Recourse Loans

Buying apartment buildings at auction can be scary. I was involved in a 160-unit building going for $2.1 million. To win the bid and have the option to buy the building, I had to put 10% down on the spot. This was nonrefundable and would close the rest of the deal in 30 days, which made the logistics very tricky. I needed to have my lending lined up. How could I do this if I do not know whether I would even get the deal?

We won the bid that day for $2.1 million. I needed to leave a cashier's check for $210,000 — nonrefundable. Equally scary, I had only 29 days to find the rest of the money needed to close the deal.

| | | |
|---|---|---|
| ☐ | Paid | $2.1 million |
| ☐ | Sold | $3.4 million |
| | | Profit: $1.3 million |

In a non-recourse loan, borrowers are not responsible for the money they borrow from banks. All they need to do is return the keys and say, "Sorry. It didn't work out." This happened frequently during the economic downturn of 2010 to 2013, and many of these apartment complexes ended up with Freddie Mac and Sallie Mae. It is not these agencies' job to run apartment buildings. They just want them off their books as fast as possible.

So, people like me buy from them. I found a place for approximately $3 million, turned it around, fixed it up, and created a wonderful community for the residents. I later sold it for $6.5 million.

| | | |
|---|---|---|
| ☐ | Contract | $6.72 million |
| ☐ | Paid | $2.72 million |
| ☐ | Debt/Refi | $3.2 million |
| ☐ | Prepay | $350,000 |
| ☐ | Brokerage | $175,000 |
| ☐ | Closing | $150,000 |
| | | Profit: $2.845 million (approximately) |

## Management Companies

I got into the rhythm with multi-family properties just as I had with single-family homes. I had bought one single-family house every 30 days, and decided to buy an apartment building every 90 days, which I accomplished for nearly five straight years. I used the power of syndication to bring people together and offer them partial equity on apartment complexes for sale. I spent so much time in the apartment business that I decided to expand the small management company I had groomed over a few years. Doing that successfully leveraged my experiences.

Eventually, my company grew to over 225 people and I earned  a good reputation for asset management. It was easy to pick up customers. Our company grew to 7,000 apartment units. To accommodate that, I bought and operated from a 55,000-square-feet office building. It had so much available space that I created an educational seminar on the real estate business, teaching others how to prepare for retirement, have their own assets pay for their successes, and create generational wealth. I taught real estate investing, from houses to apartment buildings, and eventually, commercial  real estate. Sharing my knowledge and insights in this way was extremely rewarding.

CHAPTER 8

# Retail Shopping Centers/Strip Centers

I remember leaving my apartment complex one morning, tired and worn down. I went to my local Starbucks and enjoyed a cup of coffee on the patio. While sitting there, I asked myself: *Why can't I own a retail shopping center strip like this one?* I was ready to try something new. It's worth repeating: every three to five years, we should at least think about reinventing ourselves. I think this is a good idea as long as you can build on your successes in the future.

In my case, this started with parlaying my success with single-family houses into the apartment business. Now, I bring all those experiences into retail strip shopping centers. It all began at Starbucks when I asked myself, *How do I actually do that?* Our goals of buying grand pieces of real estate sometimes seem so far out of reach that it's overwhelming. We don't want to think about it at all. Instead, I urge you to ask, *How did I do it before?*

When I was just starting out, I lived in an apartment, and went rollerblading every day. I would fly past house after house after house, asking myself, *How did they come to own this house? What do I have to do to own one?*

I began taking the right classes and baby steps forward to figure out how to get my first house, and then I accomplished this goal. I bought more than 300 houses and kept more than 200 of them for my rental portfolio. I also began a real estate flipping business, so occasionally the rental portfolio dips to 150 houses, but I'm always replenishing my stock.

I set lofty goals and when I met them, I decided it was time to leave the housing business and go into the apartment business, using the same curiosity and the same goal-setting methods. I bought my first apartment building, then 17 more — over 2,000 apartment units in all. After another three to five years, I started asking myself, *What's next? How do I carry this experience over into retail?* Retail is very different, yet there are many common denominators. I asked myself, *How, how, how?* I was driven to read as many books on retail shopping centers as I could, to find a mentor in this niche, and to the join the right associations on shopping centers — with the same process I followed in all my other ventures.

I scoured the Internet, and took the first concrete step by calling up a brokerage shop that specialized in selling shopping centers. I took their broker out for lunch. We hit it off and I learned more about shopping centers. We came up with a plan, and before I knew it, I had purchased my first shopping center, in Wyoming.

Previously, I had been within easy driving distance of all the real estate I ever owned. I found it appealing to be able to get to my property quickly. Now I was buying a retail shopping center 2,000 miles away. I decided it was worth it, because retail is very different from both single- and multi-family housing in that tenants are creditworthy — the tenants I like to pursue — and we have triple net leases. This decision was the right one. The numbers got bigger as the value of the land increased beyond its original purchase price.

When considering a retail property of this size, it's important to remember a simple idea: If you can figure out how to bring 20% to 30% of the down payment, then you are already 70% to 80% funded, because if it's a good deal, a bank will lend to you. A triple net lease is a whole new game. It's a landlord's dream coming from the housing business. I was an expert at fixing this and fixing that and paying, paying, and paying — while watching these expenses eat away the profit. Don't get me wrong; housing is a great business, but there are easier ways of making money in real estate. I found this to be true with triple net leases.

What is a triple net lease? Basically, your tenant pays for insurance, all of the maintenance, and taxes, the things that eat away our profits in the housing business. In retail, these issues are precisely measurable. You know what your tax rate will usually be, and you know what your insurance will cost. Since I am not the one personally paying for the expenses when something breaks, I know what it will cost me: $0 — read the lease. I got a phone call from a tenant a few weeks ago complaining that his front door would not close. He assumed I would fix it, but I told them to read the lease, which clearly states that problems of this type are the tenant's responsibility. Triple net leases have been a game changer for me because the tenants do 99% of everything.

Another thing that I like about strip shopping centers is that financial analysis reporting is very easy. An analysis report for apartments can be very long. My profit and loss statements are around 40 pages for each apartment complex, but my profit and loss statement for my Wyoming center is just one page! This is because I no longer have those extra expenses. Tenants pay for them, not me. It's much more predictable and safer, as far as I'm concerned. As a result, this is a scalable business — and it's important, as we grow in our real estate careers, that we get involved in investible real estate.

Houses are investible, but are sold to a mom and pop, or small business owner; in retail shopping centers, on the other hand, major corporations are the ones looking to do business. These centers are easier to trade, and they have more measurable financial results, to the point that you can almost trade it back and forth, like a stock. Over the last nine months, I have bought six shopping centers. I think I buy one every month and a half, much like my strategy with complexes. The analysis is easier, more banks seem to lend on this kind of product, and the returns are steady. Sometimes the returns in the shopping center business are not as lucrative as maybe the C-class apartment complex business, but this is better because it involves less risk.

Some of my tenants include Allstate and Farmers Insurance, national coffee franchises, dentists, chiropractors, nail salons, Little Caesar's Pizza, Domino's Pizza, Subway, Quiznos, AT&T, and T-Mobile: Fortune 500 companies. They sign a lease and pay for it as long as they are in business, regardless of whether they keep this particular store open or not. Looking back, I realize there were times when I did not collect the rent from my homes or apartment units, but this does not seem to happen in the strip shopping center business.

Another thing I love is the incredible opportunity to increase the value of the center when we bring in new tenants. Let's say I have a 10,000-square-foot shopping center with a dentist. They are geographically trapped, unable to move, and expect local clientele to move with them to the next location. I'm devoted to doing service-sector shopping center deals that can't be disrupted by outsourcing or the Internet — it's hard to replace a sandwich shop, pizza place, or nail salon on Amazon.

They also bring a huge opportunity to increase the center's value. A Starbucks or AT&T brings tremendous credibility. They enter with their promise to pay the lease, all their expenses, and their taxes and maintenance. It makes the center more valuable for the next buyer and brings more security to you.

Ask yourself: Would you rather buy a shopping center that had an AT&T, T-Mobile, and a Starbucks in it, or would you rather buy another center that just had a dentist, a massage place, and a nail salon? Of course, you go for the bigger names. Those names increase the valuations of your shopping center by millions. They bring a huge opportunity to make a lot more money, and I think you can make that money faster.

The adage of location, location, location, is absolutely true, especially in the retail shopping center business. The name of the game is to find a busy corner. You want corners, corners, corners. Hard corners. Corners where you have to turn right or a left. Corners where there is major traffic. You want traffic: car counts. I bought a center in Houston last month that 100,000 cars pass by every day. This kind of property will only become more valuable. It's in a major thoroughfare and the highways are always being widened. Location and traffic are the name of the game, and we get to reposition, too.

## How to Make a Quick Million

(*using an old formula*)

If it's broken, then fix it. We do this with houses, apartments — and why not — shopping centers. Rehabbing, redeveloping, and repositioning an old center can bring a huge opportunity. You can also attract higher-quality names to your center to make your profits grow exponentially. Popular, national brands mean the valuation of a shopping center skyrockets. I've purchased centers that were 50% vacant and filled them up using the following formula.

| | | |
|---|---|---|
| ☐ | Paid | $1 million |
| ☐ | Tenant Allowance | $100,000 |
| ☐ | Sold | $350,000 |

Profit: $1 million

Down Payment: $300,000

I purchased a 1500 square-foot, half-empty shopping center in Boise, Idaho. Basically, I bought it at half price because we buy shopping centers based on how much profit they produce. All I had to do was find three more tenants to increase the value by over a million dollars. I did not find those three tenants; my leasing broker did.

A leasing broker specializes in finding tenants. They charge a 4% to 6% commission based on the value of the lease. Most leases are for five years. Here's one example: my broker placed a national cell phone company that paid $18 a square foot in a storefront that had 1,500 feet.

1,500 x $18 = $2,700 a month

$2,700 x 60 months = $162,000 x 5% commission = $8,100

This might sound like a lot to pay a broker; however, based on the going sales price in the area, that one lease increased the value of my shopping center by $400,000. The agent didn't stop there, however, but found two more leases for three new tenants: a massage parlor and insurance company.

I once invested in a shopping center in Houston that had a nail salon, a sun tanning business, a salon, a Turkish restaurant, and a wine shop. I implemented the number one rule when buying shopping centers. I visited all of the stores. I got pedicures. I ate Greek food. I got my hair done. I picked up a bottle of wine for dinner. This would be part of a day's work for me, going under cover to test my tenants. Parking is another issue. Four to five spots per 1,000 square feet of retail space usually works well, but I like to hear first-hand from my tenants and their staff on this topic.

I also enjoy shopping centers because I get to exercise my cash flowing mindset through other people's businesses. I get to see their sales, gross incomes, and business systems, and explore franchises that I would never see the inside of if I did not own the shopping center. I get phone calls from franchisees, which is very educational. You might be surprised at how well some of these companies do.

I recently signed a lease with a major payday loan business, which is extremely interesting, and taught me so much. I also signed a deal with a Mediterranean restaurant and a Taco Del Mar franchise. All these businesses make my day much more exciting, which in turn further enriches and inspires my cash flowing mindset. In fact, I am looking into buying franchises and putting them into my own shopping centers. This is the layout of the center now:

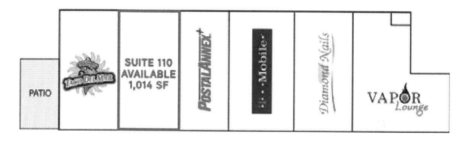

I had lunch with a friend recently who develops shopping centers for a living. He pulled out a clean sheet of white paper and showed me how his business works, and he was curious about why I wasn't doing the same. He folded the paper into four squares and explained that this is what makes him millions of dollars each project: he buys an acre of land on a busy road that has a great future. He then builds four plain vanilla boxes (or storefronts); he actually told me that he installs "three walls with a glass front."

He said it's a win-win for him and the buyer. He makes his money up front and the buyer will receive a full center with tenants that will pay out a 12% return on their money. By the time dessert came, he had shown me one more thing. He pulled out another piece of paper but didn't fold it. He said it represented one storefront, otherwise known as single-tenant pad site, the out-parcels we see all the time in the parking lots of a major grocer or a stand-alone business on a popular corner.

My friend had just gotten a call from a major hamburger franchise looking for another location in his area. Having a written agreement from the tenant, all that my friend needed to do was find and prepare the best site. It was his choice to hire a general contractor and build the structure, or just to prepare and prep the lot and let the national franchise handle the rest. Either way, the plans were coming from the franchisor.

As I bid him farewell, he told me that I was halfway there already, since I was buying half-empty shopping centers at a discount.

He said I was ready for development because I was doing it already because shopping centers have signs that say, "Build to Suit."

## My First Center

Who would have thought that my first shopping center purchase would be in Wyoming, a state I had never even visited? By the end of my first trip there, I was the proud owner of a center that had just lost its major tenant, Radio Shack. I was attracted because I knew the seller would owner-finance the deal and need to sell at a 20% discount to cover the lost space and income. The shopping center was in a great location in a popular part of town, and I was confident that we could fill the vacant spot. In doing so, I would instantly increase the value of the center by $300,000. It took a little longer than I thought, until a hearing aid company with 80 locations moved in.

My partner, Danny, passed out flyers, and one eventually turned into a lead and then, a tenant. I interviewed brokers that same week. Blain, who represented the owner, insisted on driving us all over town. He gave us the strategic layout and a map of traffic flow throughout town. He pointed to a strip shopping center in front of a Super Walmart. We later learned that Blain was the proud owner of a national sandwich shop franchise. He told us that he managed the center for the owner, whom he hadn't seen in 10 years

The owner lived in California and never visited because it ran smoothly, and it always remained full. I said to myself, *How nice. I want to be that guy in California.* Danny and I ended up purchasing that center, too. We are very happy to have both assets, and recently put them both on the market as a package with a $2 million markup. Meanwhile, the cash flow is fantastic.

CHAPTER 9

# Cash Flow Mindset

Many of us dream of making lots of money, whether it's $1 million, $5 million, or even $100 million. Growing up, I had those fantasies, too. I dreamed about the end result but not what I had to do to make it happen. By the time I figured this out and decided the direction I wanted to go, quite frankly, I was running out of time, searching for scalable businesses that could grow fast. I was desperate to get out of my current job and on with my life.

Sometimes, people figure out what they want but don't have enough time to make it happen. I see this with many others, and I remember when I played guitar and dreamed of being a rock star, or invested in properties and thought I could become a maverick international investor, or real estate magnate. I knew what I wanted, not how to make it happen. The fact of the matter is that we have a bigger problem today: five million dollars today is not worth what a million dollars was a decade ago. What does that mean? It means we are running out of time. We need to speed up the process and leverage our time through a Cash Flow Mindset.

I created the following formula that gives a new twist on leveraging time:

Passive Income

\+ Chunks of Cash

<u>+ Multiple Businesses</u>

= A Cash Flow Mindset Philosophy

This is one of the reasons why the Cash Flow Mindset is so alien and distant: no one really told us about it. Our parents never understood the concept because it was never taught in school. Baby Boomers and Gen-Xers were brought up to believe in buying stocks, annuities, and retirement accounts, which would grow from dividends and reinvestments. That is 40 years of time and a lot of education that is failing to help tens of millions of people retire.

Now, millennials are seeking solutions. They are what I call the Tablet Generation — children 13 years old and up — looking for a richer quality of life based on financial formulas that are archaic, outdated, and doomed to fail. Most people born after 1980 have no clue what cash flow is, what dividends are, or how to attain monthly income by not working but by investing passively. Imagine that you have an ATM machine in your private room and all you have to do is walk up to it, press a button — you don't even need to stick your card into it —and out pops money every single time. Imagine what you could do, what you would become, and what you could accomplish. Total financial freedom is an idea that keeps me going. It feeds off my excitement and the possibilities of what life has in store for me each and every day. With this freedom, what can I do and whom can I help?

Sometimes that ATM machine breaks down, which is why we need at least seven, if not a dozen, of them. If you are a small business owner, entrepreneur, real estate investor, or just an investor, you still need multiple sources of passive income. After 20 years of my journey, of falling off the path and getting right back on, I discovered a successful road map to riches that I would like to share with you.

## The Road Map

So many of us find a job, and then learn a skill. Entrepreneurs find a job, learn a skill, and quit to start the same business on their own. What happened here? Instead of one source of income, our entrepreneur now has two: one from the job and one from the business. If you do not have a job or a business, you can borrow money and start one, or buy your first house and start a business the way I did.

I tracked all the places I've been over the last 20 years, and came up with a formula for instant and successful real estate results. By combining and buying existing businesses (other real estate assets), I was able to leverage my position with the bank and borrow more debt. So, unlike the case in other businesses, where a startup might not be able to find enough funds, I used my balance sheet with many different assets on it. I borrowed more debt to buy new assets, which is a classic example of product line extension, creating value for myself along with new revenue streams.

1.  Houses — hold and rent
2.  Houses — flip for chunks of cash
3.  Apartments — hold and rent
4.  Apartments — flip for chunks of cash
5.  Shopping centers — hold and rent
6.  Money lending — be the bank
7.  Education — business courses and books
8.  Real estate notes
9.  Single tenant, triple net leases, hard corners
10. Stocks, bonds, and commodities
11. Exit strategies for an easier life, and a method of leaving a strong estate plan for the ones you love

It's important to build multiple businesses so that you can have multiple sources of income. A collection of revenue streams will give you the courage, confidence, and funds to build an empire and protect yourself in downturns. There will also be times when one business is born and another dies. A problem we are experiencing around the year 2020 is that employees bring only one or two skills to a job. When economies change, they find themselves unemployed. They are victims of economic disruption, replaced with more efficient technology.

By using existing revenue streams as a base, it's easier to go bigger. This strategy will keep you focused on money-making activities and prevent you from wasting time on businesses that are either on overdrive, collecting cash flow, or sleepy and not doing much at all. Each day, I actively focus on the business that generates money.

My first business, with its open outcry commodity markets, yelling and screaming, buying low, selling high, and taking orders, lasted 15 years, yet was replaced nearly overnight by electronic trading screens. Eventually, those screens replaced thousands and thousands of people. We all lost our jobs, businesses, and for some, our lifestyles. The world is always changing, and we have to adapt by maneuvering and positioning our businesses.

For me, it did not matter because I had multiple businesses providing multiple sources of income. Losing my commodity-trading job simply gave me more time to concentrate on my Cash Flow Mindset. I had rental houses, a house-flipping business, an apartment business, and an apartment-flipping business. I built up even more when I had time to concentrate on discovering more methods of passive income and cash flow from real estate and other businesses. You can't catch a fish without bait, and I always kept my hook in the water.

## Prepare to Jump from Asset to Asset

When our businesses stall for whatever reason — markets are hot, or prices are too high — and investment properties are few and far between, we can switch to another product and create wealth from our buffet of businesses. If houses cost too much, then maybe, just maybe, there are other opportunities, like apartment buildings and shopping centers. Or, if prices are too high, we can switch into a different asset.

Maybe now is a better time to move money out of one sector and into another. We see this all the time in stocks, bonds, and commodities; however, since real estate is not traded by stockbrokers, commodity brokers, and financial advisors, we hear less about these options. It's a good idea to have a dozen options through a dozen businesses that you can choose from. This way, you can always focus and grow your Cash Flow Mindset philosophy by switching in and out of sectors, each of which is a business you've created for yourself. Positioning and profiting can take time, but a well-thought-out plan can change your life forever.

Moving from one asset to another also has another benefit. Once you get the hang of making money, it is easy, and even easier when things are good and everyone is making money. It's when things are bad that people start losing money. At that point, our approach to money needs to change: How do we keep our money in bad times?

For example, as I write this, I am surrounded by an overbuilt apartment environment. It's easy to see if you understand that sometimes it can take up to four years to break ground and start building. This means that even when things are overbuilt, developers will continue building right into a recession, or create a bubble that bursts. The lesson is that we have two choices: do nothing and sit out the downturn, waiting for this asset to crash, which seems to happen every 10 years or so, or sell all the apartments in your portfolio and buy them back cheaper years later. The latter is how I keep my money when things are bad.

Eventually, as we go through this process, we find we do less and less, yet control more and more. This is the perfect definition of leverage.

You find yourself leveraging your money and your irreplaceable time. In fact, you manipulate time. You can choose, as you mature, where you want to spend your time, because one thing is certain: As you get older, you will be less able to do things physically. Growing into your Cash Flow Mindset and lifestyle mindset over the years thus becomes an art involving debt, equity, and cash flow allocations. If you want to shift from houses to a drugstore center, or a Walgreens single-tenant building, it's easy. This is asset swapping, selling the houses and buying the single-tenant building tax-free. It all comes down to where you are with your Cash Flow Mindset philosophy.

If I leave the country for a few months, I might do fewer rehabs and focus more on passive cash flow. If I need a down payment for another property, I will focus more on flipping a house or apartment complex. If a new business opportunity arises, I might sell a property or two to buy that business.

There is a reason I chose the order I explained to you: your real estate transactions will become larger and more valuable. The dollar amounts will be greater, along with your cash flows. Some start off with a $50,000 house, then buy a $500,000 apartment complex, and then a $5 million shopping center. It makes perfect sense to gradually work yourself into this Cash Flow Mindset. You will find that it thickens your skin and builds your confidence, and — most importantly — teaches you to be a good steward over your cash flow streams as you grow and test new businesses.

The process soon takes on a life of its own. Investors always look for ideas that generate a ton of cash flow, and will seek your expertise. By the end of the process, you'll always have enough down payment money because you will have multiple streams of income. The same team that runs my house portfolio also runs my house-flipping division. The same team that runs my apartment business also runs my apartment-flipping business. The same team that oversees my financials also runs my lending business. This overlap provides continuity and wisdom.

Do you get it? You will take on more responsibility, so it's important to monitor your numbers. I use multiple software products, with dashboards to chart the growth of my cash flows. As you work your way up, you will find that you spend more time with your CPA and attorneys than you do out in the field looking for good investments — by then, you will have other people doing that for you.

## Cash Flow Mindset Philosophy

Again, this is the Cash Flow Mindset philosophy: as you mature, you learn to let others do what they are best at, and you stop trying to do everything on your own. Pay attention to the rule of 72:

| Rate or Return | Years to Double |
|---|---|
| 25% | 2.8 |
| 20% | 3.6 |
| 15% | 4.8 |
| 10% | 7.2 |

Monitor the velocity of your money. It's easy to get started, get rich, and stay rich if you remember the Cash Flow Mindset principles. Be a good steward of money, respect the funds you raise, and remember how hard your investors worked for their money. My primary focus is on how fast I can return their capital. By doing this, their ROI explodes with growth. When you improve their return on capital, they will call you for your next deal. When they finally have nothing left in the deal, then their returns from you are infinite, and you are now a rock star in their eyes.

# Conclusion

## Courage

We all are born with the powers of greatness and achievement.

Some of us are more sensitive and attuned to these qualities than others. Therefore, some people are quicker at getting from Point A to Point B. This is part of our life's challenge: to find and succeed in this and to get a little bit better each day. For me, this meant jumping into a third-world country and failing miserably. I chased a childhood dream of creating a business in a far-off land, in search of a better life. The problem was, I had no direction. I had a poor plan, and failed miserably.

I went back into corporate America in an attempt to bury my entrepreneurial spirit and accept an identity that was not mine. I was beaten down, convinced that I needed more training before going off on my own again. If not for 9/11 — a disastrous national tragedy that changed the course of my life — I probably would have hidden and suffered there forever, not trusting my instincts or Cash Flow Mindset desires. In demonstrating courage, however, I learned that it's never too late to change course.

# Starting

*(is more important than a plan)*

I was afraid to trust myself. I was scared to take a chance on a newly dreamed-up, small idea for a future, big business. Each time I saw the economy sailing into head winds, I clung to my job. There is a saying: "Fool me once, shame on you. Fool me twice, shame on me." Losing my courage once was one thing, but losing it twice was a reminder of who I truly was and what I was meant to do on this earth. When you get knocked off the trail twice, it helps put things in perspective, and reminds us that it is possible to change course.

How do we find courage and faith? Here is how: you must always be your best, even when you are not. Call it self-talk or a fantasy, but it is your life, the movie you direct and star in, and we only have one take, so let's get it right. In my house remodeling and apartment complex businesses, I've learned that projects are always more successful when the right preparations have been made. A paint job always looks better if the walls are first floated, taped, and textured correctly.

With that in mind, I have found that a morning routine is vital to success in creating a Cash Flow Mindset and cash flow businesses. I spend between one and three hours every morning stretching, meditating, exercising, and reviewing my plans. I learned a long time ago that the story we tell ourselves is the one we most believe. It's a good idea to tell yourself great stories in the morning and set yourself up for success. Other mornings, when I am short on time, I run through a five-minute plan:

1.  Think about what makes me happy and how I can make other people happy

2.  Visualize my future

3.  Go over my plan

I encourage you to wake up earlier, write down your goals and plans, and run through them in your mind every morning until they become part of you. You will find that in two to three weeks, you will not be chasing your goals, but they will be chasing you. They'll pop up throughout the day. It will be easier to connect the dots as small victories bring you closer to your goals.

Schedule your goals on your calendar and make time for yourself. Make it both personal and a business, and get everything done. Every morning, I run through a half dozen of my businesses in my head. I visualize myself making the phone calls and succeeding. Every morning, run through six to 12 possible scenarios. I can tell you the figures on my balance sheet, profit and loss, and cash flow. I know where I will make money, as well as where I won't. This is all part of my morning practice. I know where to focus, effectively concentrating my time and effort. I also know when it is time to rest and conserve energy.

I loved the first house I bought. I wanted to live in it for the rest of my life. My wife had other plans and as I look back, I see that she was right. Five years after buying it, we moved to a more suitable area to raise our children closer to their schools and the heart of town. How did we continue to grow bigger and get out of our comfort zone, and add another zero towards our net worth?

I devote two days each week to review, in what I call the Saturday Review and Sunday Planning. On Saturday, I look at the current week's calendar on my iPhone. I review what was successfully completed, and what was not. I immediately move the unsuccessful activities to the upcoming week. I go back over my victories and accomplishments for that week. On Sunday, I begin planning for the upcoming week and schedule what I carried over from the prior week.

I also look at my hundred-goal list for the entire year, and assign a time slot on my calendar to a few of them.

Then, the first thing every morning, I go through my events for the day ahead. Planning and taking time to relax or rejuvenate are vital. All too often, I see people stuck in the same rut, and their mind needs some down time. As my business grew, I learned that growing twice as big required doing half as much physically! It's important to control your adrenaline. Down time can be very profitable, especially if you always contemplate, "What am I doing and how can I do better?"

I crushed my 10-year goal in less than one year and learned that when we try to do too much, too fast, we run into trouble. Pace yourself, and as you improve, do more. Plan your future; don't let it plan you.

Acknowledging daily achievements with rewards and celebrations is important. I created a date day with my wife, where we go out for a couple's massage, special lunches, special dinners, or buy special gifts to celebrate our accomplishments. This is also a reminder of our struggles when we were down to our last $1,200 in San Francisco, of having two cars with no air conditioning in Houston, and when I lost my business in Venezuela. When my spirit flew out of me and I was down in the dumps.

I am reminded of watching a jaguar while on safari in Africa. The jaguar conserves energy by sleeping in a tree for hours and hours. When it comes time to hunt, though, it will take off between 75 and 90 miles an hour for less than one minute. It needs to eat, it needs to win, and it needs to conserve energy when it is not hungry or hunting. That jaguar is thinking about what must be done while it's resting, just like you. You need to know and contemplate your goals, and you need a plan for success. It is imperative that you are at your best and that you tell yourself that you are, even when you aren't. Whatever is holding you back, whatever you are afraid of, you must find a way to break through. Practice positive affirmations that inspire you to move forward.

There was a time when I was afraid to buy a single house, and then somehow, I bought more than 300. There also was a time when I was afraid to buy my first apartment complex, and I bought 17 more, with 2,000 apartment units. After that, I was afraid to buy shopping centers — yet I recently purchased over half a dozen. The point is that obstacles are the best possible things for us. They become our incentives! If it were not for these obstacles, I never would have figured out the how-to aspect of creating successful business results. Just like a fruit has thick skin around the soft, sweet inner core, so does a business. It has its obstacles and entry barriers around successful cash flows and profitable operations.

It took me a while to figure out that there will be no end-result without a well-calculated plan. I remember my first job selling shirts from my family's clothing line when I was 13. I had dreams of opening a chain of women's clothing stores. Eventually, I realized I was just a salesperson without a plan. Later, as a musician, I dreamed of owning and running a record company — but I could not figure out the systems and the operations, so I remained on the creative side only.

Use your time wisely. Why manage 20 houses if you can manage one apartment building that has 250 units and generates more profit? At the end of the day, you need to be the person willing to do the work, willing to make a change and lead from the front, no matter what you want to do. Every action has risk. It's up to you to decide if it's worth it. Remember, look for an advantage and be patient. Most of all, be careful what you wish for — because you will probably get it.

The great entrepreneur Jim Rohn has a saying: "It's not what you get. It's the person you become." In my experience, the more you get, the more appreciative you become. This is the true value in life — it's not just what's in your bank account, or your cash flows. Finally, I believe that the more things we try, the greater our chances of success. Be more accountable. One way to do this is to schedule time to think. Take that time; tell yourself that you will do nothing but think, and then go deep about a specific situation — use the machine between your ears that we call a brain.

## Pinning Donkey Tails in the Dark

*(don't play it…)*

Many of us want to go in many different directions at the same time. We think we can be in more places than one, but I quickly learned that this is impossible, and nothing will get done if we continue. A map, a roadmap, a plan: call it what you want, but without one, you will need to be lucky. Why leave everything to luck when you do not have to? If your business is well thought out, well organized, well capitalized, and has a well-grounded and innovative business plan, you will be better off than if you just wing it. You will be better off than your competitors, too.

I would not recommend building a house without blueprints. Similarly, I would not recommend buying an apartment building without an exit strategy, and I surely would not recommend purchasing a business without prior success in the one that they want to purchase. I laid out the evolution of my working history and blueprint, starting with a small business, then buying houses, apartments, and shopping centers, then building houses and focusing on business development, and then starting a lending business.

Clearly, I've learned that the bigger you get, the more money you will make, and the more time you will need to work *on* your business — not *in* your business. Pretend you are looking down from an airplane, scrutinizing and assessing your entire operation. This method has worked well for me; a lot of it comes out of my morning practices while I am meditating and planning. If I am not actually on a plane, I visualize what it would be like looking down, because scalability is the name of the game.

If you want to grow your cash flows and multiply your businesses, you will need superior concentration and focus, as well as opportunity, and courage to act when the opportunity arises. When I built my first business, not only did I not have a good plan, but I quickly learned that the plan I had was not scalable. I did not set up my product line correctly and could not grow it. When I discovered this, I found the courage to keep moving forward and develop a better plan.

To start with the end in mind sounds like a good idea, but how hard is that to actually implement? Starting with the end in mind, or seeing a vision of what can be, if you are good and planned your work, most likely you will get what you are going after — because you have the advantage. The people who want it the most usually stay in the longest and achieve their dreams and goals. They have a vision of what the finish line looks like. Successful investors always know the true value of what they want to buy and have an exit strategy or end in mind.

You have a plan; you know what it is and what it looks like so you will know when you achieve it. The danger here is thinking too small. I often see people succeed in business and cash flows, but they could've been much bigger, even huge. They meant well and they thought big, but they didn't think big enough. Instead of loading up their pipeline with new deals, they only concentrated on what they had accumulated. I spent years buying single-family houses — that was my universe. It was all I knew, because it was the focus of the only class I ever took in real estate.

The problem was that years of buying and selling houses was not enough to support my lifestyle, for me to say I had arrived. It was not enough to fulfill my dreams. This is why it is a good idea to always try making the next deal bigger than the last one. A good friend of mine who owns 7,000 apartment units has a saying:

"Why not add another zero onto a transaction?"

This is his way of reminding us to think bigger. When you catch on, you will understand what it truly means to have cash flow. You will realize that all wealthy investors are looking for cash flow appreciating assets. This is like being in a situation where everyone around you knows what's happening, and you are the last to discover it. They all know that time will pass by, and if they can gather these assets, collect, hold, nourish, take care of, and respect them, only then will their assets continue to grow, and their owners will grow into grander, healthier, and richer lifestyles.

There are many reasons why seasoned investors have more cash flow and assets. Primarily, it's because they are experts. They went through the evolution of real estate investing and pursue core assets towards the end of their investing career. Core assets are irreplaceable pieces of real estate: that hard corner by the busiest intersection in your town, or property sitting at the corner of an exit off a major highway carrying nearly half a million cars every single day. It's a piece of dirt with a new building or an old building, but definitely a replaceable building as people's needs and tastes change. Like a plant, you are either growing or dying. You need to understand that you should keep going for bigger deals and swapping up, or you will become complacent, and — hopefully not! — lazy.

Continue to build relationships with influential people. As your deals get bigger, so does the sophistication of your true friendships. Magic starts to happen and a gravitational pull starts to occur; things get easier when you succeed. Your ability to solve problems is rewarded with bigger transactions and more money — that's the goal. If you can master the velocity of your assets, move into bigger deals, and control debt, money from depreciation and leverage will flow into your hands. You will have lots of opportunities to fine tune your abilities and redefine your knowledge along the way. Remember to make the lessons clear and precise.

I spent many years studying real estate theory. Much of it boils down to seven simple steps that are broken down and easy to understand: a blueprint for wealth.

1. Income — Money that comes in
2. Expenses — Money that goes out
3. NOI — Money left over
4. Debt — Money you borrow
5. Leverage — Money used to magnify more
6. Depreciation — Money you don't pay taxes on
7. Phantom Income — Other money you don't pay taxes on

## Keep Climbing

*(take that next step...)*

I predicted a commercial real estate crash that made me millions of dollars. I was not comfortable buying my first apartment building, or shopping center, but the timing was right and it was time to do the right thing. It takes guts to buy when everyone else is selling, but it's important take a chance and try something new. I had to go through some phases to make these connections, and build the foundation one step at a time. Whether that new thing is marriage; starting your first business; or buying your first house, apartment building, office building, or shopping center; I believe the human spirit can prevail. I believe in the Cash Flow Mindset that helped make all these things possible in my life.

I also believe in education. Never stop learning, because new ideas are all around us, all the time. Take seminars, read books, and listen to podcasts. Most importantly, implement what you hear, read, or see to build a Cash Flow Mindset business. There is no greater honor than bettering yourself for the people you love or want to help.

Your mind, sitting comfortably between your ears, can quickly take you to lofty places. You need to hang around people who want to grow and excel and build just as you do. Before you know it, they become a support group that will hold you accountable. You should be curious, always looking for new and exciting ways to improve — not just for yourself, but for others, too. When it comes to fear and failure, you only experience both when you give up. So the most important thing to do is . . .

**Dust yourself off, and do it again.**

Stay open to change! It's the human spirit's job to always keep improving! Pay attention to your philosophy, principles, and money, because if you have one of the three, the other two will follow — and then your driving force will kick into overdrive. Each and every one of us has a driving force, and we should live up to our potential. The next time you find something broken, why not fix it and see if you can make a profit? Leave it better than you found it.

There will always be a higher step in the staircase of life. Believing in your Cash Flow Mindset makes that next step much easier. Create your business systems. One of my missions is to impact millions of people with my ideas. Its starts with just a few people, but together, we can use these methods ourselves and pass them along to our families and friends. Once we do, the world will be a better place.

# About the Author

A lan Schnur is a first-class real estate investor based in Houston who is changing the way people buy real estate, create cash flow, and trust their entrepreneurial drive to obtain true financial freedom and a richer, fuller life.

Over the years, he has put together an impressive real estate portfolio while building a company that has more than 200 employees. With partners, Alan has bought more than 2,000 apartment units and managed more than 7,000 units, along with hundreds of single-family houses. He owns numerous medical, office, and warehouse buildings, along with a dozen shopping centers around the United States, and builds multi-million-dollar custom homes.

Through books, presentations, seminars, and consultations, Alan shares his Cashflow Mindset with anyone seeking true financial freedom.

Alan travels the world as a mentor and speaker. He has lectured at Harvard University, and recently published the second edition of his book, Creating Your Own Real Estate Cash Machine.

Alan is a civic-minded family man, living with his wife and son in the heart of Houston. He and his business partner were honored by Houston Mayor Parker and the Houston City Council for their commitment to providing affordable, quality housing to families in need.

## Alan's Story

After an early career in finance and business, Alan's desire to gain control over his own financial destiny and create true financial freedom for himself and his family led him to learn about real estate investing through whatever free information he could find. The knowledge he gained turned his life around and led him to develop the Cashflow Mindset of investing strategies and methods learned from personal experience.

After investing in a few single-family rental homes, Alan realized he could apply the same principles and techniques to larger properties and achieve much greater financial returns. He invested in apartment units and later worked his way into other types of commercial real estate, as well as ventures including private lending and investing in student housing.

Today, he is known around the country not only for creating massive amounts of monthly cashflow through investment properties, but also for sharing his expertise with others who seek the same financial freedom.

## Other Interests

Implementing his Cashflow Mindset has given Alan and his family the time and resources to focus on other interests, including world travel. He has been many places, including the Taj Mahal in India; the Swiss Alps and Himalaya mountains; Mt. Fuji in Japan and the top of Mt. Kilimanjaro (19,341 feet) in Tanzania, Africa; the scenic trails of northern Thailand and the Golden Triangle (where Thailand, Burma, and Laos converge); Australia's Outback (on foot and by camel); and the outer edge of the Great Barrier Reef. These awe-inspiring adventures further shape and propel Alan's philosophy of success in both business and in life.

## Contact Information:

email: alanschnur@gmail.com
phone: 713-503-5908
website: https://www.alanschnur.com

# A|B|S

82740296R00065

Made in the USA
Columbia, SC
07 December 2017